Miniature
CAKES

Miniature CAKES

Lindsay John Bradshaw

MEREHURST PRESS
LONDON

I would like to thank the publishers for giving me the opportunity to write and create designs for this unusually interesting subject of sugarcraft in miniature, in particular Jane Donovan for her continuing help and advice.
Published 1988 by Merehurst Press
5 Great James Street
London WC1N 3DA

Co-published in Australia and New Zealand by Child & Associates,
Unit C, 5 Skyline Place, Frenchs Forest, 2086, Australia

ISBN 0 948075 98 8

Managing Editor: Deborah Gray
Proof Reader: Julia Thorley
Designer: Richard Slater
Cover Design by Clive Dorman
Photography: Lindsay John Bradshaw
Typesetting by:
Vision Typesetting, Manchester
Colour separation by Fotographics Ltd, London-Hong Kong
Printed by Henri Proost, Turnhout, Belgium

Contents

Introduction

Making miniature cakes is every bit as interesting as making full-size cakes, and even more fun. In fact, it is a real challenge to see how small you can actually make the various items of decoration and to come up with miniature substitutes for special features and ornaments.

This book is aimed at providing many new and original cake design ideas, enabling you to create colourful and attractive miniature delights. Although the book is entitled Miniature Cakes, all the ideas can quickly and easily be adapted to suit cakes of any size by simply enlarging the templates and designs given with the instructions for each cake. Conversely, the cakes can be reduced in size still further to make really tiny miniature cakes. Choose your own favourite recipes for the cake bases and fillings, and

just follow the advice given on selecting small tins and preparing cakes for decoration. All the techniques and methods referred to in the book are exactly the same as those used for larger cakes, just remember while you are baking and decorating them to think small . . . think miniature.

Miniature cakes and novelties make mouthwatering gifts for children to give to grandparents, are ideal as special place settings for parties and celebrations, or they can be used as stunning table centrepieces for dinners, buffets or wedding receptions. The size of these cakes makes them particularly well suited to give to senior citizens, people who live on their own, or others who require only a small gift. Another novel application of the miniature cake theme is to make a replica of an actual celebration cake and then

give it as edible take-home gift or as a souvenir of a special day. People who were unable to attend the function would also be pleased to receive a miniature cake!

Your finished miniature creations can then be presented in specially made presentation boxes. There are instructions on how to make these, along with ideas for edible and non-edible gift-tags in the first section of the book. These finishing touches personalize the gifts and protect the cake if you are placing it on display for sale or exhibition purposes.

Miniature cakes, then, will solve all your gift problems and will provide you with a wealth of ideas when it comes to sending along a cake for the craft fair or the cake stall. Above all, enjoy making them, and remember, miniature cakes are fun!

Foreword

It is always sweet news to the sugar industry when another book is published which promotes the art of sugarcraft in such an attractive and appealing way. There is no doubt a tremendous amount of interest and growth in all types of sugar work is now taking place and *Miniature Cakes* is the latest in a long line of excellent books dealing with a subject which brings endless hours of pleasure to many thousands of people.

I never ceased to be amazed at the creativity, artistry and high degree of skill involved in sugarcraft and Lindsay John Bradshaw has succeeded in scaling new heights in this unique and charming form of cake decoration.

Every joyful occasion is marked by an appropriate cake. This book has opened up many new opportunities to say "congratulations", "thank you", "good luck" or simply "here is something special". People love to receive a gift which is delightful, delicious and is a result of hours of painstaking work by someone who derives a great deal of pleasure from this enchanting pastime.

Lindsay John has unlocked a whole new world of enjoyment through *Miniature Cakes* and is part of a trend towards a return to the good things in life. I hope this book encourages more people to practise the rewarding art of sugarcraft and I wish the author every success.

Gerard Bithell
PUBLIC AFFAIRS MANAGER
THE SUGAR BUREAU

Making and Preparing Cakes

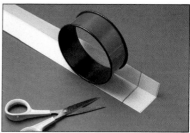

To measure the length of paper required to line the sides of the hoop, position the seam or join of the metal hoop at one end of the paper strip and carefully roll the hoop along the length of the paper. Where the seam of the hoop next touches the paper will indicate the required length, then allow about 1cm ($\frac{3}{8}$in) overlap and cut to size.

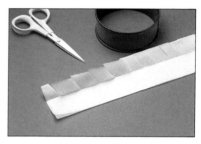

Snip along the smallest side of the fold using scissors. Make the cuts at an angle so that they overlap when positioned in the hoop.

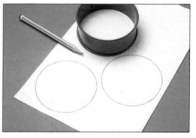

For the base liner, place the hoop on a double thickness of greaseproof (waxed) paper and draw around the inside of the hoop as shown. Cut out the circles just inside the line to allow for the thickness of the tin, and ensure a good fit.

The prepared greaseproof (waxed) paper liners are then positioned neatly in the hoops; remember to place the hoop onto a cardboard

Making cakes is a matter of personal preference, everyone has their own favourite recipe, which may be used to make miniature cakes. These may be plain sponge, chocolate cake or rich fruit cake, all of which are made using the normal method, but using smaller quantities. Simply halve the amounts of all the ingredients used in the standard recipe, or quarter the amounts to make a really small cake.

Baking times will be reduced, especially for rich fruit cakes. The small cakes described below made in 7.5cm (3in) hoops take about 20 minutes for a victoria sponge-type mixture, and about $1\frac{1}{2}$ hours for a rich fruit cake.

The main difference between baking ordinary and miniature cakes is in the selection of small tins.

Selection of Cake Tins

There are a number of different small cake tins that can be used to bake miniature cakes. Depending on the size of the cakes and the number required, you could bake a sheet of cake and cut out the required shapes. This method is obviously better suited to straight sided units that will not create waste cake. If you do find that you have cake trimmings, try making trifles, country cakes, frangipan tartlets with the sponge cake waste and rum truffles with the fruited cake crumbs.

Here we see a selection of tins which are ideal for baking miniature cakes.

Crumpet or muffin hoops, available from cookshops and department stores. These measure approximately 7.5cm (3in) in diameter, and are 3cm ($1\frac{1}{4}$in) deep. Yorkshire pudding tins are an ideal size. Build up the sides to make deeper cakes using a band of thin card, and then line in the usual way.

Pudding tins or foils make a good shape for the domed miniature cakes featured. Once baked and cooled the upside-down pudding shape can be cut, layered and trimmed as required.

Conventional cake tins are probably best for square and oblong shaped cakes. Sheets or slabs of cake can be baked in these and used for cutting out unusual shapes, or shapes that are unavailable as tins. Using a rectangular tin, for instance, you can bake a full cake and cut it into two smaller square shapes. If you do not require two cakes, freeze or store one for later use.

Lining Tins

Use double thickness greaseproof (waxed) paper for all tin lining.

To line the small hoops, fold along one edge of the greaseproof (waxed) paper about 15–20mm ($\frac{1}{2}$–$\frac{3}{4}$in) wide. Position the hoop on its side with one edge of the hoop on the fold. Mark the depth of the hoop as shown, and draw a line along the length of the paper, then cut along the line.

and greaseproof (waxed) paper-lined sheet tray or Swiss roll tray before lining and depositing filling into them. Cardboard is used as a base for your hoops to give added protection to the mixture during baking, and to help create a good even bake.

To line square or rectangular tins, place the tin on a double thickness of greaseproof (waxed) paper and draw around the base shape as shown. Position the tin so as to overlap the paper by about 6mm (¼in) on two edges; this will allow for the thickness of the tin when the paper is cut out.

For the sides, fold 15–20mm (½–¾in) along the longest edge of the paper sheet. Place the tin on its side with one edge on the paper fold. Mark the depth of the tin and draw a line; then cut along the line.

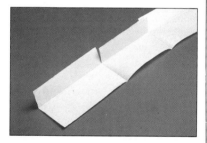

Take the inside measurements of the sides of the tin (either using a ruler, or by placing the tin on the paper and marking off) and fold the paper as shown to correspond with the dimensions. Cut along the shortest folds on two opposite sides.

Position the side and base liners in the tin.

Preparation of Cakes for Decoration

Baked cakes which have been made in muffin hoops as described earlier. Leave the greaseproof (waxed) lining paper on the baked cake until the last minute before decoration. This helps to keep the cake fresh and to retain a good shape while also reducing the risk of damage to the cake.

Chocolate cake made in a rectangular-shaped tin. The depth of the baked cake is about 3cm (1¼in).

Plain cake baked in the same tin.

Storage

After baking, the cakes should be allowed to cool slightly and then should be transferred onto a cooling wire. The cake bases should be stored for at least 12 hours (but no more than 24 hours) before cutting, layering and decoration commences. This storage period allows the crumb to close a little and the cake as a whole to firm up, thus enabling easier handling.

Sheets of cake that are baked level to the top of the tray are best left in the sheet trays and stored one on top of the other, the top sheet being reversed and separated from the other with a sheet of grease-proof (waxed) paper. If only one sheet of cake is being stored, a lightly weighted tray can be placed on top to close the crumb whilst the cake is firming up.

Removal of Crust

Before cutting, layering or covering of any kind takes place it is normal practice to remove the crust or 'skin' as it is often called. The crust is easily removed by drawing the back edge of a long knife across the cake; this way the thin crust is removed without damaging the cake. With smaller units such as sandwich-type bases the crust is probably better removed with a sharp serrated knife. Depending upon the type of cake and sometimes the bake, a loose crust can be removed by rubbing and gently peeling with the fingers.

Removed crust can be used like normal cake crumbs in a wide range of products such as truffles, trifles or frangipan tartlets.

During Preparation

During preparation of the cake for finishing, always keep the bases covered to prevent the cake drying out. This can be done by covering with polythene sheets, or by placing the cakes in polythene bags. Alternatively cover with a clean, moist tea-towel or an upturned handbowl. Never leave cakes exposed to the atmosphere, especially when they have cut surfaces.

Cutting and Slicing

To achieve even and accurate slicing, which will eventually help with good layering, use special cutting boards. These are pieces of wood or polypropylene cut to various thicknesses. Place a cutting board at each side of the unit to be sliced, then position a sharp knife resting on the boards.

Cut through the cake to create accurate layers.

Once the crust has been removed, the cakes can then be layered and shaped. It can be seen that one rectangular sheet, when trimmed of all edges will produce two small square cakes. It is important to trim enough cake from the edges to remove dark crust and create flat, straight sides.

Filling and Layering

Obviously many various creams, conserves and fillings are going to be used to layer the cakes. Spread

an even layer of cream or jam on the cake layer using a palette knife. Work the cream to just short of the edge of the cake. Replace the layers of cake in the order that they were cut, unless you are dealing with an unevenly shaped cake. A slanted cake, for instance, may be rectified by replacing the cake layers in a different position.

Buttercream or Filling Cream
Gently beat the cream to a smooth consistency to remove small lumps or a crusted surface. Adjust the consistency if necessary by warming over warm water, or by the addition of a small amount of warm liquid.

Conserves and Piping Jellies
Mix gently with a wooden spoon to remove any lumps. If the jam is particularly stiff, add a small amount of stock syrup or water and mix gently to a smooth consistency. Do not beat.

Apricot Jam (Jelly)
It is normal practice for fruit cake and marzipan work to use boiled apricot jam (jelly). For short shelf life products such as genoese and sandwich-type units the cakes will be made and finished for only a relatively short period of time, and consumed within a few days, and it should not therefore be necessary to boil the jam (jelly) for this type of finishing. This also applies to battenburg, fondant gateau and other marzipan coverings on genoese units.

Cleanliness

Organize your work and keep a clean work surface. After removing crust, slicing and trimming, remove all traces of cake crumbs. If these adhere to the cake or get mixed into the filling cream the appearance of the cake will be affected.

Trimming and Shaping

For a couple of the cakes featured in the book – the tortoise and parasol – the base dome shape is achieved by baking the cake in a pudding tin as described earlier.

The cooled, baked cake can then be cut and layered with jam (jelly) and filling cream as shown.

Before commencing to shape the cake it is advisable to chill the layered unit for 30 minutes to 1 hour to firm up the cake and fillings. This chilling makes shaping easier. Use a good, sharp knife to trim and shape the cake; wiping the blade on a clean cloth and dipping the blade into warm water before each cut helps to achieve a clean, neat appearance. Trim off a little at a time until the desired shape is created. Remove all excess crumbs before commencing with any covering or decoration.

Preparing Fruit Cakes

Allow the cakes to cool for about 15 minutes after baking, then liberally brush with a mixture of equal parts sugar syrup and rum. There should not be any need to prick the surface of the cake, simply brush the liquor on top, allowing it to penetrate slowly into the cake, leaving the lining paper in position. This addition of

syrup will close the crumb a little and make a firmer, yet moister eating cake. Make sugar syrup by boiling a small amount of water and stirring in granulated sugar until it becomes a thin syrup. When the cake has cooled completely, wrap in greaseproof (waxed) paper and store in a cool, dry place until required.

Rich fruit cakes for miniature work are baked in small hoops or tins as described earlier. For slabs of fruit cake, use your normal square or rectangular cake tins but reduce the amount of cake mixture by approximately half to produce a shallow cake. Baking times for smaller cakes will be considerably reduced. The baked cake after storing and maturing can then be cut to the required size.

Use the conventional method of marzipanning a cake as for larger cakes. Roll out the marzipan using a little icing sugar. Brush the top of the cake with boiled apricot jam (jelly) and place the cake centrally on the marzipan. Trim off any excess with a knife.

Roll out a long, narrow strip of marzipan slightly larger than the depth and circumference of the cake. Roll-up the marzipan Swiss roll fashion and then unroll it around the sides of the cake which

have already been coated in apricot (jelly). Trim and seal at the join.

Trim off any excess marzipan around the top edge using a knife. Cut towards the centre of the cake top so as not to peel back the marzipan on the sides of the cake.

For a square or oblong cake, use the method described for covering the top of a round cake with marzipan. For the sides, roll out a rectangle of marzipan slightly wider than the width of the cake and as long as the depth of four cake sides. Position the cake coated with apricot jam (jelly) on its side and trim round neatly.

Turn the cake over to the next side and again place on the marzipan and trim round; repeat on the remaining two sides.

Neaten the marzipan on the sides using plastic smoothers to produce the prepared cake marzipanned on all four sides.

Cake Cards

Small cake cards on which to decorate your miniature cakes can be purchased from good sugarcraft shops or through mail order suppliers. However, small cake cards are only usually manufactured in round and square shapes. If you need an unusual shape not available in the shops, it is quite simple to make your own card to the exact size and shape required.

1 Trace the required shape from the many templates provided in the book onto thin white card. Cut out the shape neatly using scissors, or, for difficult shapes, a craft knife may be better.
Using glue, stick the cut-out shape onto a piece of silver or gold board covering foil which is available in rolls from sugarcraft shops. Cut around the shape leaving a rim of foil about 12mm (½in). Snip the rim of foil at short intervals to ensure a neat finish, similar to preparing greaseproof (waxed) paper for lining a cake tin. Apply glue to the back of the foil rim and then fold over and secure firmly all the way round the edge. The board is now ready for use.

2 Here we see a selection of home-made cake cards in various shapes and sizes, covered in both silver and gold foil. These have all been made as described above.

Presentation Boxes

Presentation boxes may be purchased ready-made, or for a more personal touch, make your own. They are easy and fun to make, and you can co-ordinate the cake theme and colour to the box and gift tag.

1 Glue a piece of attractive gift wrapping paper onto a sheet of thin card. Avoid using gift wrapping foil, as paper is easier to work with.

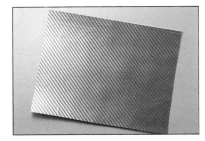

2 Turn the card over and trace on the box template from page 14. Mark the lines that are to be folded with a faint dotted line.

3 Cut out around the template and the window circle. Score along the dotted lines with a pair of scissors held firm against a ruler. Carefully bend and fold along the dotted lines.
Glue a square of clear acetate on the inside of the box over the window circle. Acetate is available from art shops; look for the type found in wedding cake ornament boxes.
At the places indicated on the template, glue the box, holding for a while or securing with paper clips until set (remove paper clips before placing the cake inside).

4 The finished box ready for use. Many attractive designs of wrapping paper are available; save any off-cuts to make gift tags as shown below.

Gift Tags

To personalize your miniature cakes as you give them for gifts and presents, try making some edible gift tags. They are easy and fun to make, so use your imagination to create more ideas of your own. Colour some sugarpaste with edible paste colours, then roll out thinly. Cut out shapes using food cutters, fancy tins, or a knife and ruler. You could even rib-roll the sugarpaste before you cut out the shapes to create interesting textures on the gift tags. Using the small end of a No 2 or No 3 piping tube as a cutter, cut out a small hole in each tag to allow you to finish them with a coloured thread.

1 Having cut out the shapes, allow them to dry and then edge them with piped line designs using a No1 or No0 tube with coloured royal icing. Thread gold or silver gift tie or narrow, coloured ribbon through the tags, finishing with attractive bows. Use the tie to attach the tags to the cakes or boxes.

4 The valentine chocolate box is shown here with a matching personalized edible gift tag.

2 Using a No1 or No0 tube with coloured royal icing, pipe inscriptions, greetings messages or names onto the gift tags as required. Please note the gift tie is not edible. If you prefer a less fragile gift tag, make it from gift wrap-covered card as described for the boxes. Cut out a rectangle, fold in half and thread with a gift tie.

3 A delightful miniature anniversary cake in its own presentation box with matching tag – a perfect gift!

Presentation Box

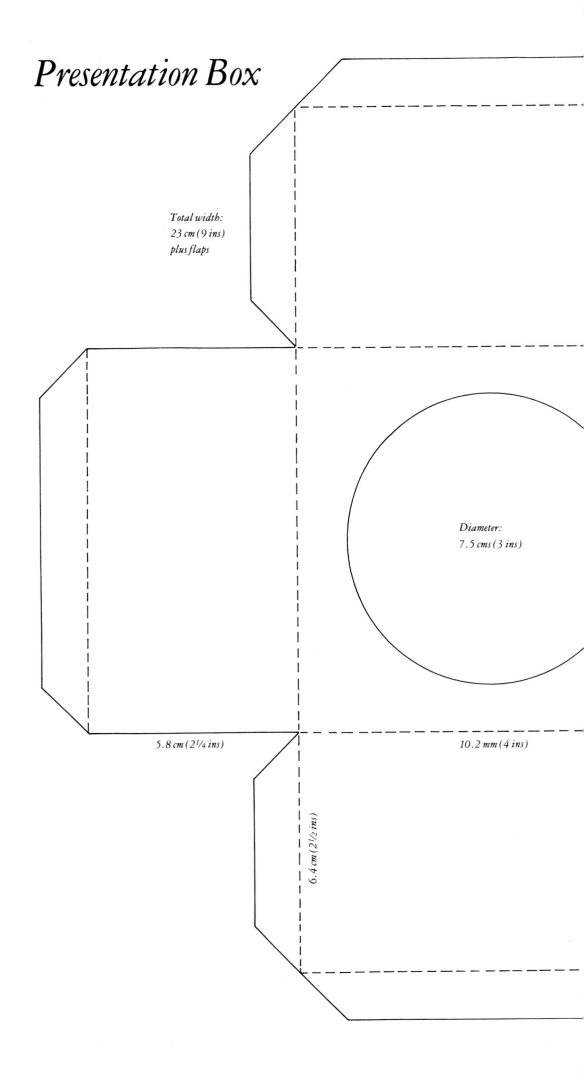

Total width:
23 cm (9 ins)
plus flaps

Diameter:
7.5 cms (3 ins)

5.8 cm (2¼ ins)

10.2 mm (4 ins)

6.4 cm (2½ ins)

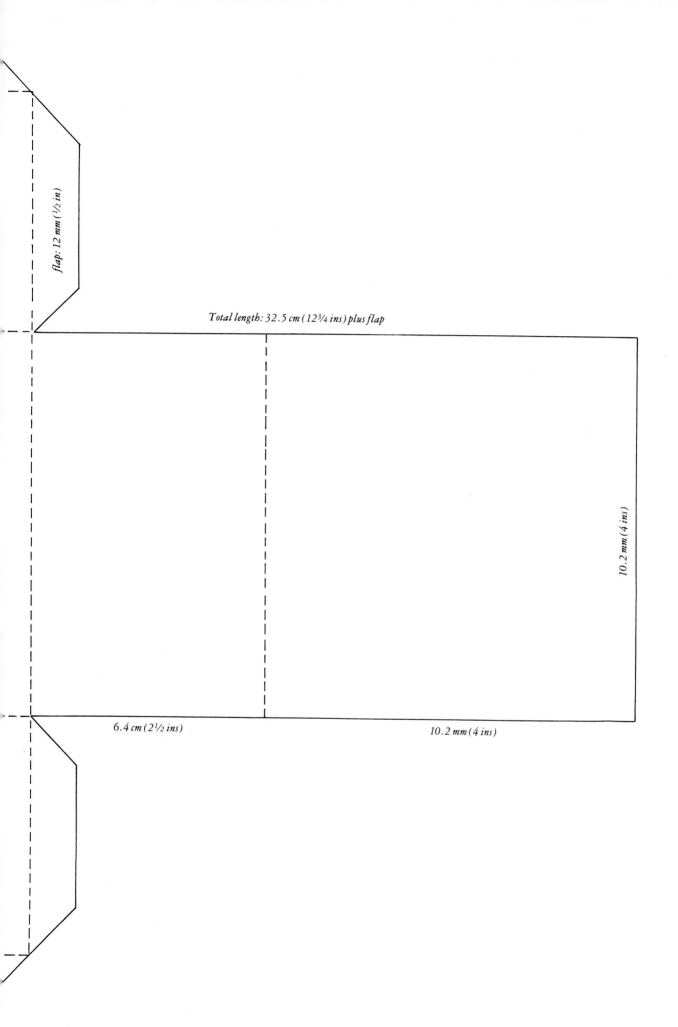

flap: 12 mm (½ in)

Total length: 32.5 cm (12¾ ins) plus flap

10.2 mm (4 ins)

6.4 cm (2½ ins)

10.2 mm (4 ins)

Happy Clown

Approximate
Height
of Cake
5cm (2in)

Approximate
Diameter
of Cake
9.5cm (3¾in)

The happy smile on this clown's face,
along with his colourful hat and bow-tie,
make this an ideal cake for a party,
take-home gift.

1 Cover the basic round cake top and sides with pinky-peach coloured sugarpaste. Allow to firm up a little.

2 Using royal icing, attach coloured sweets around the base of the cake. Make a large, round red nose for the clown from marzipan.

3 Make the clown's mouth by rolling out a long sausage of red marzipan. Form the roll into a circle sticking the ends together with egg white. Squeeze the circle in the centre and press together to make the mouth.

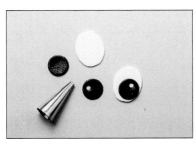

4 Cut out small ovals of thinly rolled, white sugarpaste. Stick onto these small circles of black sugarpaste or marzipan made using the large end of metal piping tubes. A small circle of the black marzipan has been removed with a piping tube; this creates a highlight effect on the eyes.

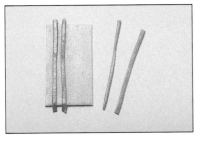

5 For the hat, roll out some pink marzipan or sugarpaste and then lay strips of thinly rolled, blue paste over the top; use a little egg white if necessary to stick the strips.

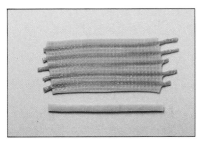

6 Roll over the prepared paste with a boxwood roller or ribbed roller to create a more interesting texture and pattern. Make a strip of pink marzipan for the hat brim.

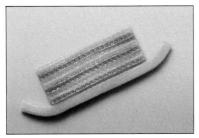

7 Cut out the hat shape using the templates provided. Attach the hat brim with egg white.

8 A flower for the hat is made by thinly rolling out some white sugarpaste. Cut out some small, triangular shapes as shown. Pinch two ends of the triangles together to form a petal. Stick five of these petals together with egg white and add a coloured centre. Make leaves by forming tiny carrot-shaped pieces of green marzipan, flatten them between polythene sheets and mark the veins (while still under polythene) with a small knife or modelling tool. Attach the flower to the hat.

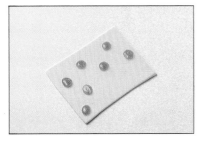

9 Prepare some spotted sugarpaste material for the bow-tie. Roll out some yellow paste and press some small balls of blue marzipan or sugarpaste onto the rolled surface. Roll out further to form a thin sheet of paste.

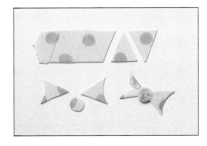

10 Cut out two triangle shapes from the spotted paste, then cut a small circle using the end of a piping tube as a cutter. Stick the two triangles and the circle together as shown to make the bow-tie. Using royal icing, attach the eyes, nose, mouth, hat and bow-tie to the prepared clown's face.

Face (cake size) 9cm (3½in) diameter

Eyes

Nose

Mouth

Bow-tie

Bow-tie

Hat

Hat brim

Flower petals

Leaf

18

Pink Cradle

Approximate
Height
of Cake
7.5cm (3in)

Approximate
Length
of Cake
7.5cm (3in)

*A delightful, easy-to-make cradle to use
as a place setting for christening
celebrations. Change the colour to suit the
occasion . . . it looks just as pretty in
pale blue.*

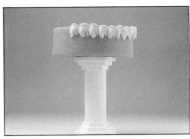

1 Cover the basic oval-shaped cake base with marzipan. Roll out the marzipan, apply some apricot jam (jelly) to the top of the cake and place the cake onto the marzipan. Cut round the oval shape and remove excess marzipan. Roll out a long strip the depth of the cradle side and attach this to the cake with apricot jam (jelly).

Place the marzipanned cake onto a support to raise it off the work surface and enable you to turn the cake around to make piping easier. Position the cake upside-down on the support and then upturn when piping is complete. Using a No57, 58 or 59 petal tube and pink-coloured royal icing, pipe petal-type shapes around the cake.

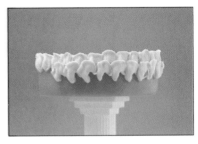

2 Pipe another row of petal shapes slightly lower than the previous row. Keep piping rows of petal shapes, until you reach the bottom (to be the top) of the cradle side. The effect creates the appearance of draped material.

3 Once the side piping is completed, the cake can be removed from the support and up-turned. Pipe a further two or three rows of petal shapes around the edge and partly onto the top of the cradle, creating a neat edge to the decoration.

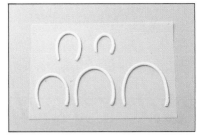

4 Make the hood of the cradle by using the templates provided. Place the templates underneath a piece of waxed paper and pipe the shapes using a No44 tube and pale pink-coloured royal icing. Allow to dry.

5 When the piped hood shapes are dry, roll out a small piece of white sugarpaste and cut out an oval shape. If you have not got a cutter, simply flatten out a ball of sugarpaste to the desired shape. Brush the marzipan on the cradle top with egg white and stick the sugarpaste piece in place. Whilst the sugarpaste is still soft, press in the graduating piped hood shapes as shown. Do not use too much pressure when inserting the piped pieces or they may break.

6 Form an oval shape of white sugarpaste to represent a body. Also make a pillow case, again from white paste. Position the pillow and body shape on the cradle, attaching with a little egg white.

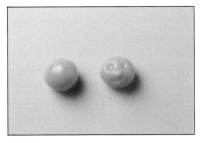

7 Make the baby's head from marzipan. Form a ball shape and then elongate into an oval shape. Using modelling tools, indent the eyes and mouth. A tiny marzipan nose is then attached.

8 For the cradle cover, thinly roll out some white sugarpaste and cut out a round, fluted circle, square off the top. The broderie-anglaise is created using fine writing tubes No0 and No1 to make attractive patterns. Pipe around the holes with white royal icing and a No00 tube. While the paste is still soft, drape the cradle cover over the baby's body shape allowing it to form the contours of the body. Decorate the cradle with tiny sugar or silk flowers and ribbon bows attached with dabs of royal icing.

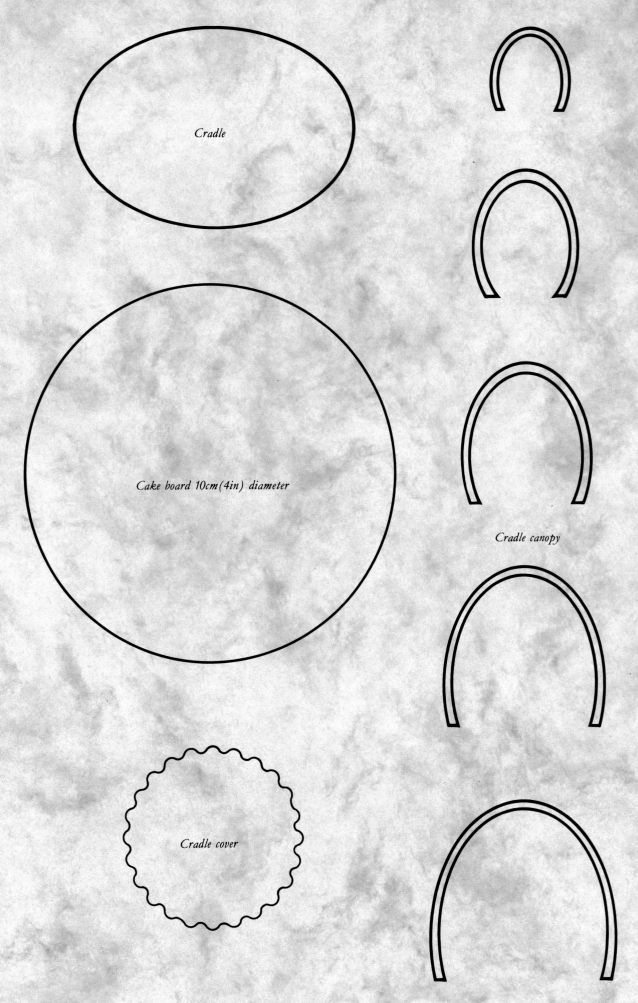

Cradle

Cake board 10cm(4in) diameter

Cradle canopy

Cradle cover

Wise Owl

Approximate
Height
of Cake
10.5cm (4¼in)

Approximate
Width
of Cake
7.5cm (3in)

*Exam success deserves a special cake, so
what better way to celebrate than with a
wise owl decorated with delicious, chocolate
buttercream.*

1 Prepare the basic sponge cake shape using the template provided. Coat all sides of the shape with chocolate buttercream.

2 Using a petal tube No57, 58 or 59, pipe petal shapes in regular rows over the sides of the coated cake to represent the feathers of the owl.

3 Using the same tube and cream, pipe two wings on the front of the owl by building-up rows of petal shapes to form the finished triangular shape.

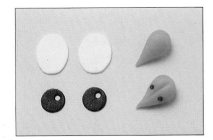

4 Thinly roll out some white sugarpaste and cut out two oval shapes for the eyes. Also cut out two small circles of black-coloured sugarpaste, removing a small hole for a highlight. The circle can be cut using the wide end of a piping tube, and the highlight using the narrow end of a No2 or 3 tube. Stick the black circles onto the white ovals with egg white. Model a beak from egg-yellow-coloured marzipan, and indent a line on the beak using a small knife or modelling tool. Two tiny balls of black marzipan inserted with the point of a cocktail stick complete the beak.

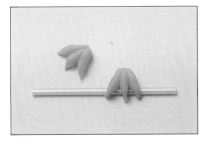

5 Mould six small carrot-shaped pieces of egg-yellow-coloured marzipan and attach together in two sets of three as shown to make the claws. Set the claws on a small piece of drinking straw to allow them to dry with a curve.

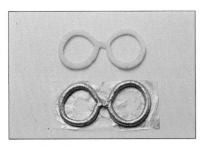

6 Model the spectacles from a thin rope of marzipan. The circular shape can be easily formed by positioning the marzipan around the wide ends of two piping tubes, securing the join with egg white. When the spectacles are dry, paint them with gold or silver food colouring.

7 Make the mortar board by cutting out a square of thinly rolled black sugarpaste or marzipan, using the templates provided as a guide to the size. Make the base of the mortar board from a ball of black paste cut in half and allowed to dry. Model a few thin strands of black paste and attach together with a little egg white to create a tassel. When dry, stick all the various parts together.

8 Attach the eyes and beak to the owl with a dab of buttercream.

9 Attach the mortar board and claws.

10 Model a small pencil from sugarpaste or marzipan along with a sugarpaste plaque on which you can pipe a name or inscription of your choice.

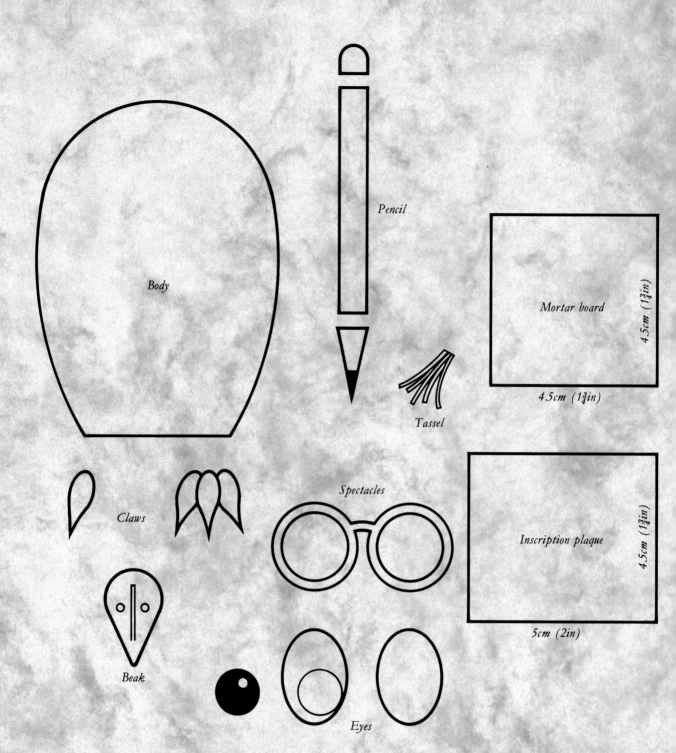

Body

Pencil

Mortar board

4.5cm (1¾in)

4.5cm (1¾in)

Tassel

Claws

Spectacles

Inscription plaque

4.5cm (1¾in)

5cm (2in)

Beak

Eyes

Rabbit in Bed

Approximate
Height
of Cake
8cm (3¼in)

Approximate
Length
of Cake
11cm (4¼in)

*This cosy, little bed with its marzipan
rabbit could be used as a birthday cake or
as a get well gift.*

1 Cover the basic cake shape with marzipan on the top and on all four sides.

2 Roll out sugarpaste to about a 3mm (⅛in) thickness; cover the top and two longest sides with the paste. This can be done in one operation by cutting a large rectangle of paste to cover the required area. Attach the paste with egg white.

3 Model a small pillow case from white sugarpaste by rolling out a fat sausage shape and cutting with scissors to the required length. Model a body shape also from white sugarpaste. Attach both pillow and body to the bed, securing with egg white.

4 To make the bed-ends, roll out two colours of marzipan; a dark brown and a caramel colour work well together. Layer several pieces of the coloured marzipan alternating the colours; use a little egg white if necessary to stick the layers together. Next, cut slices of the two-coloured marzipan and lay them side-by-side, again sticking together with egg white. Roll out the paste to create a wood-grain effect.

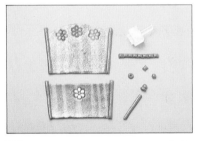

5 Using the templates provided, cut out the bed-end shapes. Attach small thin rolls of brown marzipan for the detail and finish each with a ball and a flattened ball of brown marzipan. The flower pattern on the bed-ends gives the effect of carved wood. Simply press an embossing tool into the soft marzipan, allow the shapes to dry, then paint in the flower detail using edible food colours and a fine paintbrush.

6 Model the rabbit's head. Start off with a ball shape, then elongate it into a cone. Indent the shape about half way down by pinching with the fingers. Make a central cut into the top half of the shape to form two ears. Indent the eye sockets using a modelling tool. The nose is made from a small ball of dark brown marzipan and the mouth from red marzipan modelled into a heart shape. Attach the nose and mouth with egg white. Model two hands as shown, and set aside.

7 Attach the bed-ends to the bed with a little royal icing. Position the rabbit's head on the pillow, attaching with a little egg white.

8 Prepare a presentation board by covering with pink rib-rolled marzipan. Attach the marzipan by lightly brushing the cake card with a little egg white. The edges of the marzipan can be crimped, as shown, with marzipan crimpers to give a decorative edge.

Bed-end

GET WELL SOON

Inscription plaque

Detail

Pillow

on the rabbit with white royal icing, followed by a dark brown bulb of icing. A small sugarpaste plaque piped with a suitable inscription can be attached to the base of the bed.

9 Make the bedspread by rolling out some pink sugarpaste and cutting to the required size. For the dimensions, measure the depth of the bed sides and the width of the top; and from the bed-end to just above the pillow. Make a floral pattern on the bedspread while it is still soft. Dip the embossing tool into edible petal dust, tap off the excess and indent the paste as shown. You will have to work quickly as the paste crusts quite rapidly.

11 Position the white bed cover on the bed followed by the pink bedspread and then quickly, before the paste crusts, turn back the white fluted edge. Allow the bedspread to drape over the contours of the body. Attach the modelled hands. Pipe the eyes

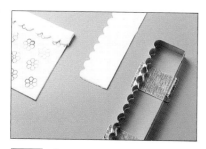

10 Cut a fluted-edged strip of white sugarpaste to form the second bed cover.

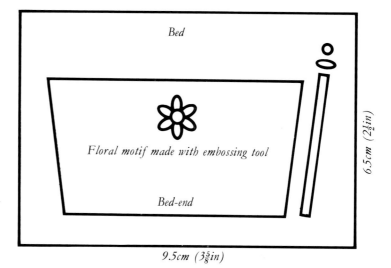

Bed

Floral motif made with embossing tool

Bed-end

6.5cm (2⅜in)

9.5cm (3⅜in)

Hands

11cm (4¼in)

Head

Marzipan rabbit

Board size

Bed cover edge (white)

15cm (6in)

Valentine
Chocolate Box

Height
of Box
3cm (1⅛in)

Maximum
Width
of Box
9.5cm (3¾in)

*A miniature valentine gift for a loved one
to treasure. This simple-to-make
sugarpaste chocolate box features embossed
and painted roses.*

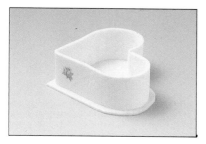

1. Roll out a long strip of white sugarpaste about 3mm (⅛in) thick. The width of the sugarpaste will be determined by the depth of your heart-shaped food cutter. The length of the strip can be calculated by holding a piece of string around the heart-shaped cutter. Using an embossing tool, mark indentations along the length of the strip. Use a rose pattern if possible, working quickly before the paste starts to crust.

4. When all the prepared sugarpaste sections are dry, remove the cutter from the heart shape and position the shaped paste on the heart-shaped base. Secure with white royal icing; use a fine paintbrush or small plastic scraper to remove any excess icing and to tidy the join.

7. Decorate the lid with a fine, roped line piped on the edge of the crimper work, use a No1 tube with pink royal icing. Pipe the inscription 'With Love' onto the lid using a No1 or No0 tube with brown royal icing.

2. Immediately after completing the embossing, roll up the strip like a Swiss roll and place into the heart-shaped cutter lined with waxed paper. Unravel the roll of paste and position it neatly around the inside of the cutter, gently pressing into the corners to create a neat finish. Allow the paste to firm up before continuing to work on this section.

5. Using a fine paintbrush and edible pink, green and brown food colourings, paint the detail on each rose. Mix edible brilliant white powder to each colour to produce delicate, pale tints of colour; the white powder also produces a better consistency of paint with which it is easier to work. Paint the rose design on the prepared sugarpaste lid.

8. Half fill the finished box with shredded red- or pink-coloured tissue paper and arrange three truffles or chocolates on top. Position the lid onto the box and present in a gift box. A greeting message on an edible gift tag personalizes the gift.

3. Using a slightly larger heart-shaped cutter than the one used previously, cut out a lid and a base for the chocolate box. The paste for the lid and base needs to be the same thickness as for the sides. Crimp the edges of both the lid and base to make a pretty decorative edge. On the lid, emboss a single rose pattern at the base of the heart near to the point.

6. Using a No1 tube with white royal icing, pipe a tiny plain shell along the edge where the side joins the base. Overpipe the white border with a fine line piped in pink royal icing using a No0 tube.

With Love

Lettering

Lid and base: make 2

*Heart size for moulding sides of box
(shape on inside of heart)*

Depth of box

3cm (1⅛in)

Jolly Jack

Approximate
Height
of Cake
13cm (5½in)

Approximate
Width
of Cake
5.5cm (2¼in)

*What a magical place setting this would
make for a children's party. Colourful
Jack looks like he has just sprung from
the box!*

Prepare the basic cake shape as a square cube of cake layered as required with buttercream and jam (jelly).

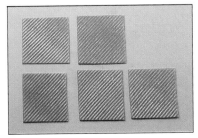

1 Using the templates provided, make the sides and lid of the box. Roll out some blue-coloured marzipan or sugarpaste to about 3mm ($\frac{1}{8}$in) thick, rib-rolling to create an interesting texture. Cut out squares of the required size. Note: two side sections are narrower than the other two, this will ensure that a perfect square is created when the box sides are attached to the cake and joined together. Allow the sections to firm up.

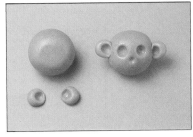

2 Model Jack's head from an oval ball of pinky-coloured marzipan. Indent the eyes and nose with a modelling tool. The ears are made from two small balls of marzipan indented with a modelling ball tool and attached to the head with egg white.

3 For the hands, roll out a sausage of marzipan and cut into small pieces. Roll each piece into a ball shape and then elongate into a carrot shape. Join four pieces together at the points, brush with a little egg white and press onto a small, flattened ball of marzipan. Bend one of the carrot shapes up to form the thumb. Make two hands.

4 Make two arms from rolls of red-coloured marzipan. Indent one end of the arm and attach the hand with a little egg white. Finish the sleeve cuffs with a fancy piped edge using yellow royal icing and a No1 tube.

5 For the spring, flatten equal-sized balls of orange- and green-coloured marzipan to form thin, circular discs. Make about three discs of each colour.

6 Make the body from a pear-shaped piece of brown marzipan. Allow to firm and then wrap a long strip of red-coloured marzipan around the body to represent the jacket. Stick the jacket to the body with egg white.

7 Cut out a collar from yellow-coloured marzipan. A large daisy flower cutter is ideal, or use a star or round fluted cutter.

8 Attach the prepared squares to the side of the cake with royal icing or buttercream.

Star template for box sides

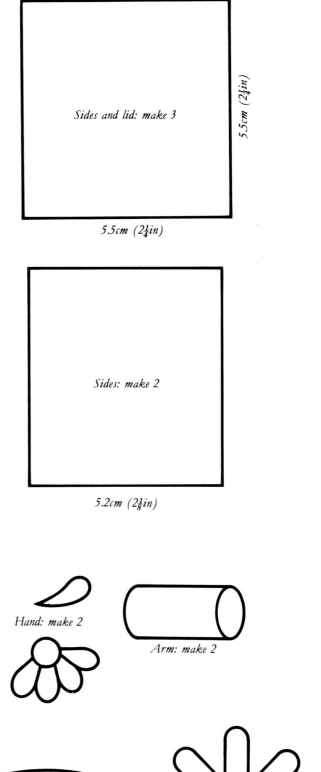

9 Brush inside the top of the box with melted chocolate to make a firm base for the figure. Brush the coloured discs with a little egg white and press together, alternating the colours as shown. Position the spring in the box, securing with a little royal icing. Attach the body to the spring, again securing with royal icing. Edge the jacket front with yellow icing as for the sleeves. Finish the prepared head with a red marzipan nose and mouth. The hair is made by pressing yellow sugarpaste through a fine sieve or tea-strainer. Small tufts of the paste are then attached to the head with a little egg white. Attach the head to the body with royal icing. Pipe the eyes on the face with white and brown royal icing.
Decorate the box with piped or cut out marzipan numerals, or a decorative edging and flower design. Jolly Jack is another novelty ideally suitable to use as a party place setting or as a going-home gift. Pipe the child's name on if you wish.

Sides and lid: make 3

5.5cm (2¼in)

5.5cm (2¼in)

Sides: make 2

5.2cm (2⅛in)

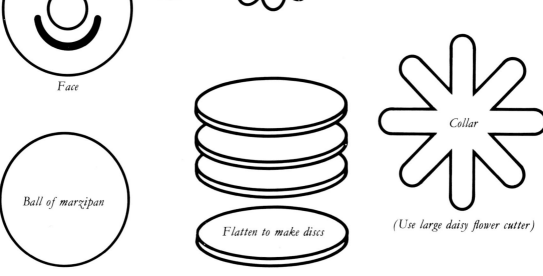

Hand: make 2

Arm: make 2

Ear

Face

Ball of marzipan

Flatten to make discs

Collar

(Use large daisy flower cutter)

Happy
Anniversary

Approximate
Height
of Cake
5cm (2in)

Approximate
Diameter
of Cake
10cm (4in)

*Make these stunning little cakes to match
the actual anniversary or celebration cake.
Each guest could then take home an
edible keepsake, which indeed would be
something different!*

1 Cover a round fruit cake with marzipan in the conventional manner, then cover with pale-coloured sugarpaste. Roll out the coloured sugarpaste to a circle, lightly brush the marzipan on the cake with spirit or egg white for adhesion and drape the paste over the cake. Work quickly before the paste begins to crust and crack; placing the miniature cake on a small container makes covering easier. Gently ease the paste down the cake side taking care not to tear the corner, smooth the pleats away gently without folding or creasing the paste, then trim off any excess around the base.

2 Peach, minty green, pink and blue colours all make attractive cakes for anniversaries.

Golden Wedding Anniversary

1 Position a peach-coloured cake on a miniature cake card and attach a narrow length of gold cake band around the bottom edge. Secure the band to the cake with a thin line of royal icing.

2 Make the icing numeral using the template provided to outline the figures. Use white royal icing and a No1 tube. Allow to dry.

3 When dry, paint the outline with gold food colouring taking care not to damage the fragile icing.

4 Flood in the numerals with peach-coloured run-icing and allow to dry.

5 For the brush embroidered floral motif, trace the design onto the cake top using the template provided. Outline the flower shape with orange-coloured royal icing, which has been very slightly softened with a drop of egg white.

6 Using a fine paintbrush, pull the piped line into the centre of the flower with short, gentle brush strokes, moistening the brush occasionally with a little egg white. Repeat the technique to form the leaves using green icing.

7 Pipe a yellow centre in each flower and then pipe on some tiny stamens with brown-coloured icing and a No0 tube. Pipe an inscription with the same icing and tube. Remove the runout numerals from the waxed paper and attach to the cake top with dabs of icing. Support the numbers with a small piece of folded cartridge paper until dry.

Templates for runout numerals

35

Ruby Wedding Anniversary

1 Prepare the cake as described, this time using pink-coloured sugarpaste. Pipe a small shell border around the base of the cake with white icing using a No44 tube.

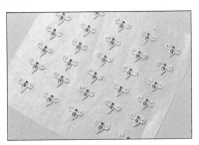

2 Make the lace pieces for the cake side decoration. Using the patterns provided, place a piece of waxed paper over them and pipe in the sequence illustrated. Use a No1 tube for all lines with pale pink, darker pink and brown icings.
Note: When making lace pieces use freshly made royal icing strengthened with a pinch of cream-of-tartar. Store the piped lace in a dry place away from any moisture and steam. Make plenty of extra pieces as they are very fragile.

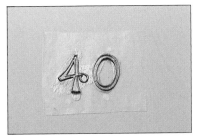

3 Make the numerals as described for the previous cake.

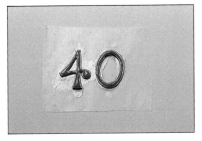

4 Flood in the outline with red-coloured run-icing. Allow to dry.

5 The prepared lace pieces are attached to the cake side starting at the base and curving upwards around the cake to finish at the top edge. A length of narrow ribbon can be attached as a template for positioning the lace and removed when finished. Carefully and gently remove the dry, lace pieces from the waxed paper. Lift them up to the cake using a fine, dry paintbrush and attach them, at an angle to the cake, as shown, with tiny dabs of royal icing. Use freshly made icing to attach the lace pieces to the cake so that they will retain their position and dry rapidly. Remove the runout numerals from the waxed paper and attach to the cake with dabs of icing.

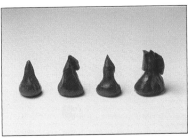

6 Model a rose from red-coloured marzipan or sugarpaste as shown in the sequence. Make the individual petals from tiny balls of paste flattened and thinned out at the edges in-between sheets of polythene.

7 Only one full rose is required; alternatively you may purchase ready made edible or silk roses.

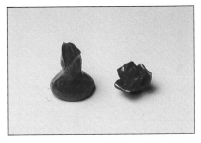

8 Model a few rose leaves from green-coloured sugarpaste. Roll some small balls of paste and then form each one into a carrot shape. Place between sheets of polythene, and flatten to thin out into leaf shapes. Whilst still between the polythene, mark the leaf veins with a small knife or modelling tool. Curve the leaves to make them look more natural, then colour with edible petal dust using orange and green tones.

9 Pipe an arrangement of lines in brown-coloured icing using a No0 tube. Position and attach the rose and leaves with royal icing.

Silver Wedding Anniversary

1 Prepare the cake as for the golden wedding anniversary, but using pale blue-coloured sugarpaste to cover the cake. Attach a narrow, silver cake band to the base and pipe a tiny plain shell using a No1 tube and white royal icing. Attach a pale blue-coloured narrow ribbon and bow.

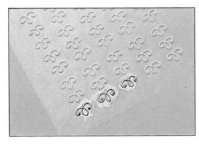

2 Make the lace pieces as previously described using white royal icing. When dry, carefully paint the lace with silver food colouring.

3 Prepare the icing numerals as described for the previous cakes.

4 Paint the outline with silver food colouring.

5 Flood in the numbers with white run-icing. Allow to dry.

6 Attach the prepared lace pieces to the cake side as previously described, just below the line of the ribbon.

7 Pipe a fine line design onto the cake top using a No0 tube and white icing. Attach three delicate, blue-coloured silk roses and a few small silver rose leaves. Finally remove the prepared runout numerals from the waxed paper and attach to the cake with dabs of royal icing.

These cakes are ideally suited to displaying in presentation boxes, as seen in the first section of the book, with gift tags carrying an appropriate greeting message.

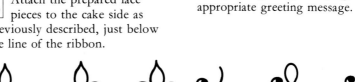

Lace pieces for ruby anniversary cake   *Lace pieces for silver anniversary cake*

Cake size 9cm (3½in) diameter

Congratulations

Lettering

Brush embroidery template

Teddy in a Car

Approximate
Height
of Cake
9cm (3½in)

Approximate
Length
of Cake
10cm (4in)

A cuddly teddy bear in a colourful motor car makes an ideal novelty for a toddler's birthday present.

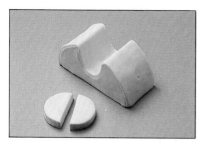

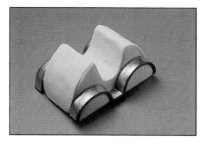

1 Cover the basic cake shape with yellow-coloured sugarpaste (the cake could be marzipanned before applying paste if desired). Cover the sides first by laying the cake, covered with apricot jam (jelly) onto the rolled out paste. Cut a long narrow strip to cover the car top and seat area. Using the same yellow paste, cut out two thick discs, then cut each in half to form semi-circular shapes from which the wheel arches will be made.

4 Allow the running boards to dry and firm-up, then paint with gold food colouring.

8 Roll out some black sugarpaste and cut out a block as shown. This block will raise the car above the cake card level and allow the wheels to be attached. Allow this block to firm-up before use.

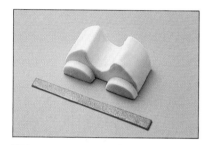

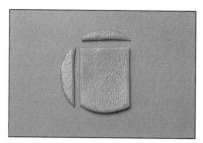

2 Attach the wheel arches to the body of the car with a little royal icing or egg white. Cut two long, narrow strips of rolled out red-coloured marzipan to form the running boards.

5 Cut out two circles of blue marzipan or sugarpaste, using the templates provided to obtain the correct size. Trim three straight edges as shown – the resulting shapes will form the bonnet and the boot of the car.

9 Spread a little royal icing on the black block and position the car body on top.

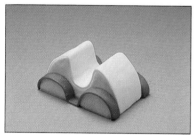

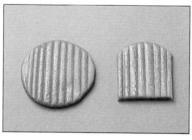

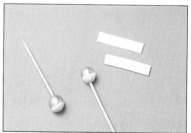

3 Attach the running boards to the wheel arches sticking them in position with egg white.

6 Using coffee-coloured marzipan or sugarpaste, make one more bonnet shape as previously described. This will form the car seat and may be rib-rolled before cutting out to create a more realistic effect.

7 Using a little egg white, attach the bonnet, boot and car seat to the body of the car.

10 Roll out some sugarpaste and cut out two number plates, pipe on an appropriate number, inscription or name. Attach the dry number plates to the car with royal icing. Roll two balls of sugarpaste and place on cocktail sticks inserted into a polystyrene block to dry. When dry, paint half of each ball with gold food colouring; these will form the headlights when positioned on the front wheel arch running board and attached with royal icing.

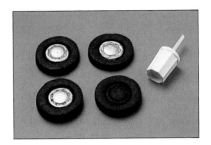

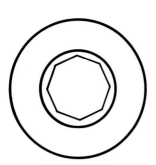

Tyre: make 4

11 Roll out some black sugarpaste or marzipan and cut out the four wheels using the template provided as a guide. The cleaned lid off a used paper correction fluid bottle indented in the wheels makes an ideal shape for the detail of the wheel centres. When dry, paint the centres of the wheels with gold food colouring. Attach the finished wheels to the car with royal icing.

12 Make the teddy bear from tan-coloured marzipan. Form a pear shape for the body and a smaller pear shape for the head. Two small balls indented with a ball tool make the ears; attach to the head with egg white. Indent the eyes with a modelling tool and pipe with white and brown royal icing. A brown marzipan nose completes the head. Model the arms and attach to the body with egg white. Stick the body in the car with egg white and attach the head.

Headlight: make 2

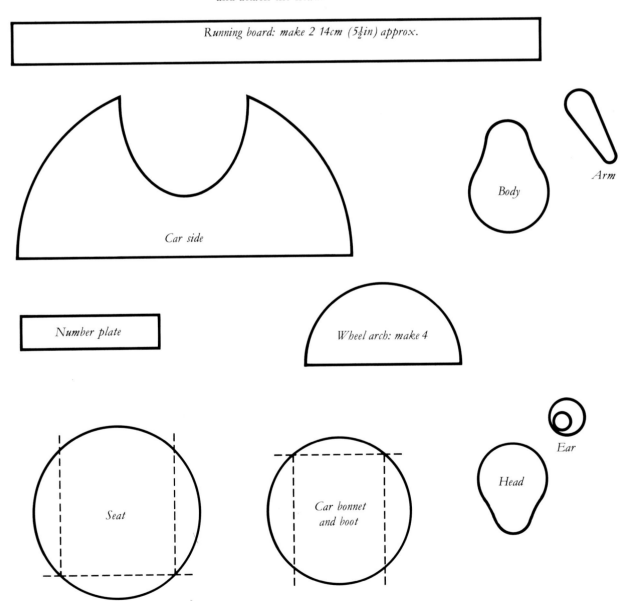

Running board: make 2 14cm (5½in) approx.

Car side

Body

Arm

Number plate

Wheel arch: make 4

Ear

Seat

Car bonnet and boot

Head

Driving Test
Pass

Approximate
Height
of Cake
5cm (2in)

Approximate
Size
of Cake
9cm (3½in)

Passing a driving test would be made an extra-special occasion with this quick-to-decorate novelty featuring a sugarpaste L plate.

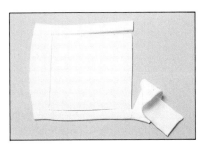

1 Prepare a basic square cake as shown. Layer a plain cake with raspberry jam (**jelly**) and buttercream or a chocolate cake with apricot jam (**jelly**) and chocolate buttercream. Place the layered cake onto a cooling wire with a piece of waxed or greaseproof paper beneath. Pour melted milk or plain (sweet or semi-sweet) chocolate over the cake and then tap the wire to encourage the excess chocolate to drain away. Remove the cake from the wire when partially set and place onto waxed or greaseproof paper until fully set. Any chocolate drippings on the waxed paper (providing they are free from crumbs) should be allowed to set fully, then peeled off the paper ready for use again.

2 Keep the coated cake on the waxed paper or transfer onto a cake card of the required size. Pipe a shell border with piping chocolate around the base of the cake using a No43 or No44 tube. Piping chocolate is made from melted chocolate slightly thickened by the addition of a few drops of cold water, piping jelly, or cream.

3 Make the L plate by thinly rolling out some white sugarpaste. Using the template provided, cut out a square of the required size.

4 Remove the excess sugarpaste to leave the square piece.

5 Make four holes in the square, one at each corner, using the narrow end of a No2 or No3 piping tube as a cutter.

6 Trace the L shape onto the square using an edible red food colour pen. Cut the L plate with an irregular line to give the appearance of the L plate being torn. Place the pieces onto waxed paper and allow to dry flat.

7 Paint the L shape with edible red food colouring and a fine paintbrush. Using a No1 tube with black-coloured royal icing, pipe on the inscription 'WELL DONE!'. Cut some short lengths of fine gold cord.

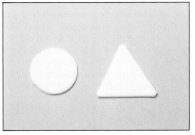

8 Next make the road signs. Thinly roll out some white sugarpaste. Using the templates provided, cut out some circles and triangles. Allow the shapes to dry.

9 Using examples of road signs from the Highway Code, paint the sugarpaste shapes using a fine paintbrush with edible food colourings. Allow to dry.
Attach the sugarpaste L plate to the cake top with melted chocolate or royal icing. Also attach the road signs to the cake sides. Thread the gold cord through the holes in the L plate and tie in a bow.

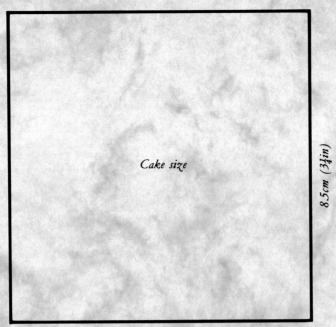

Cake size

8.5cm (3¼in)

8.5cm (3¼in)

WELLDONE!

Lettering

L plate

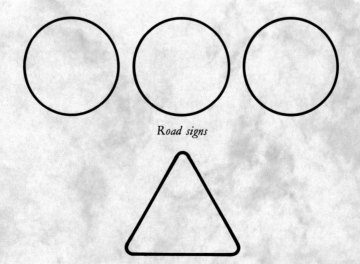

Road signs

Bride Cake

Approximate
Height
of Cake
15cm (6in)

Approximate
Diameter
of Base Cake
9.5cm (3¾in)

*Make the wedding different! Create
eyecatching centrepieces for the guests with
a miniature bride cake on each table at
the reception.*

1. Prepare the number of tiers you require by baking varying sizes of rich fruit cake in miniature tins. Add spirit to the cakes as for normal-sized wedding cakes and then marzipan the cake in the conventional manner. Ice the cakes applying two or three coats of royal icing. To make coating easier, rather than using the normal large, straight edge to flat ice your cakes, use a small, straight palette knife.

2. Using the templates provided, make runout collars for the cakes. Place the traced template under a piece of waxed paper and outline the shape using a No1 tube and white royal icing. Flood in the shapes with run-icing using a paintbrush to neaten the flow of the icing at the points and corners.

3. Allow the runout collars to dry fully in a warm, dry place.

4. When dry, pipe a picot dot edging on the edge of the runout collars using a No0 or 00 tube for the tiny dots.

5. Secure a narrow white ribbon around the cake side and pipe a plain shell around the base using a No1 tube with white royal icing. Repeat on all tiers. Make a card template from the collar design provided, and position it on the cake card as shown. Pipe a line to follow the template using a No1 tube with white icing. Remove the template and pipe a second line next to the first line. Overpipe the first line using a No0 tube. Repeat on all tiers.

6. Using the same tubes as used for the base linework, pipe the side linework design as shown. Simply mark the top edge of the cake with tiny icing dots to line-up with the joins on the base linework. Drop scallop lines onto the cake side from the dots, then overpipe. Pipe fine filigree onto the cake card using a No00 tube and white icing.

7. Attach the prepared runout collars and pipe linework on the inside edge to follow the shape of the collar. Repeat on all tiers.

8. Make miniature cake pillars to support the tiers from short pieces of wooden dowel. Attach two graduating size, small, card circles to each end of the dowel with glue; thin cake cards are ideal for this purpose. Paint the pillars with white non-toxic paint and allow to dry.

9. For a miniature top ornament, make a tiny vase from an upturned, plastic bell cake decoration from which the top has been removed to enable it to stand up. Fill the vase with an arrangement of moulded or silk flowers; use tiny, silk cake decoration flowers, wired and cut to size.

Use some tiny flowers that match the ones used in the vase to decorate the spaces between the linework at the base of each cake. Assemble the finished tiers of the cake, supporting them with the miniature cake pillars. Complete the bride cake with the vase of flowers.

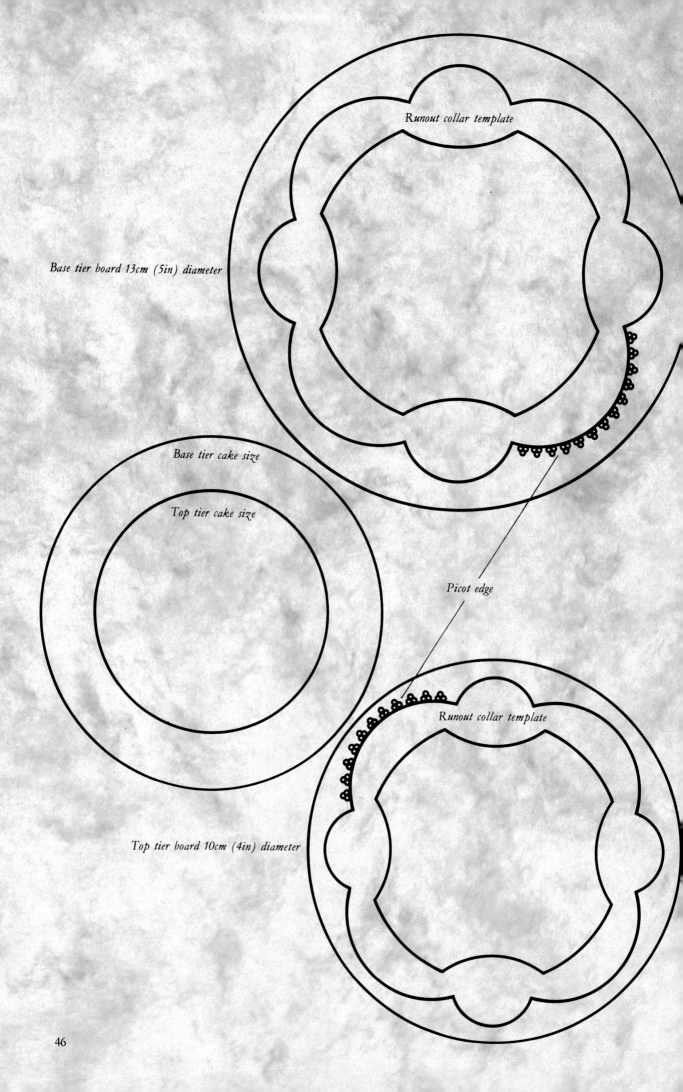

Runout collar template

Base tier board 13cm (5in) diameter

Base tier cake size

Top tier cake size

Picot edge

Runout collar template

Top tier board 10cm (4in) diameter

Rocking Horse

Approximate
Height
of Cake
8.5cm (3¹/₂in)

Approximate
Length
of Cake
11cm (4¹/₄in)

*Just like the real thing. This original
cake idea will appeal to all ages; and it is
easier to make than it appears!*

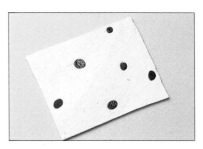

1 First prepare the covering paste. Partly mix together a small amount of grey-coloured sugarpaste (use edible black food colouring to make grey) and some white sugarpaste; do not fully mix thereby creating an interesting mottled effect. Roll out the paste and press some small balls of black-coloured sugarpaste into the flattened surface. Continue to roll out the paste pressing the black balls flat to create a sheet of spotted sugarpaste.

2 Cover the basic cake shape with marzipan and then cover with the prepared, spotted sugar-paste. Cover the narrow top first.

3 Next, cover the semi-circular side shapes first with marzipan, then with sugarpaste.

4 Roll out some red-coloured marzipan, then re-roll with a boxwood roller to create an interesting texture and pattern. Using an orchid flower cutter or the template provided, cut out the two saddle sides.

5 Using the same red, boxwood-rolled marzipan, cut out the saddle top using the template as a guide.

6 Attach the saddle pieces to the horse's body with egg white.

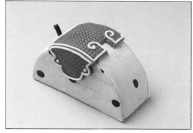

7 Model a small black tail piece and insert it into the body of the horse. Using a No2 tube, pipe the pattern detail on the saddle, allow to dry and then paint with gold food colouring.

8 Roll out some white sugarpaste to about 9mm ($\frac{3}{8}$in) thickness. Using the template provided, cut out the head shape. Allow to dry for several hours until firm. When firm enough to handle, paint on the eyes, nose and mouth with black food colouring and a fine paintbrush. To make the ears, cut out small triangle shapes of thinly rolled white sugarpaste. Tint the triangles with pink edible petal dust using a dry paintbrush. Pinch two ends of a triangle together to form the ear shape. Attach the ears to the horse with egg white.

9 To make the horse's mane, press a small amount of black-coloured marzipan through a clay gun, fine sieve or tea-strainer, leaving it attached to the sieve. Brush the back of the prepared head with egg white, then use a small knife to lift off tufts of the black marzipan from the sieve and position them on the horse's head. A small tuft of the same marzipan is attached to the end of the tail piece. Attach the finished head to the horse using royal icing.

10 Using the template provided underneath a piece of waxed paper, pipe out two rockers using a No44 tube and white royal icing. Allow to dry.

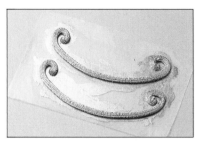

11 When dry, paint the rockers with gold food colouring and allow them to dry. Attach the finished rockers to the horse with royal icing.

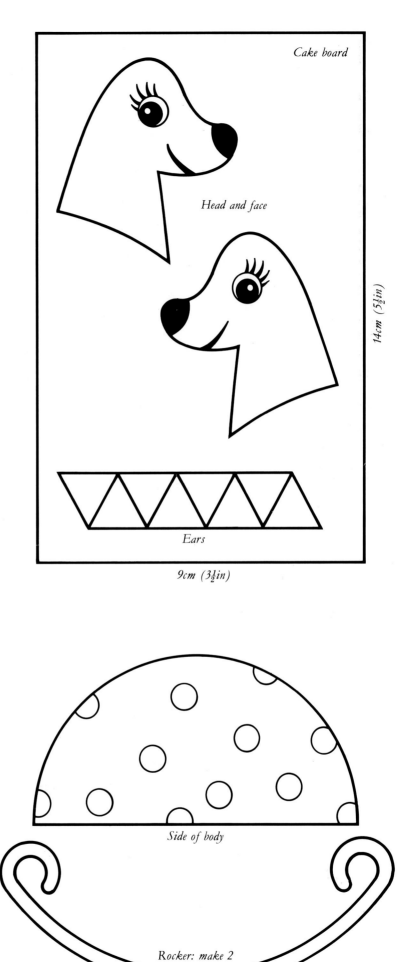

Cake board

Head and face

14cm (5½in)

Ears

9cm (3½in)

Saddle side: make 2

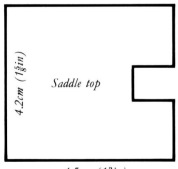

Saddle top

4.2cm (1⅝in)

4.5cm (1¾in)

Side of body

Rocker: make 2

Key of The Door

Approximate
Length
of Cake
9cm (3½in)

Approximate
Width
of Cake
5.5cm (2⅛in)

*Rich fruit cake portions each decorated
with marzipan doors and an icing key.
Edible gifts for guests at the celebration
or for those who could not attend.*

1 Partly mix together equal amounts of yellow, brown and orange marzipan or sugarpaste. Do not fully mix the colours together so as to create a wood-grain effect when the paste is rolled out.

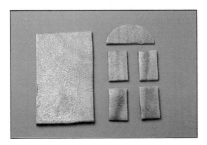

2 Roll out the paste to about a 3mm (⅛in) thickness, then cut out the shapes shown using the templates provided.

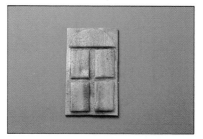

3 Position the door detail on the main oblong shape, attaching all sections with egg white. Allow to firm-up.

4 Outline the door detail and the edge of the door with lines piped using a No1 tube and orange-coloured royal icing; pipe on a 21 or 18, and a door knob. Allow to dry. When the lines have fully dried, paint the edge line, numeral and knob with silver food colouring.

5 Prepare the fruit cake portions by marzipanning the top of a fruit cake and then cutting to the required size and shape.

6 Using the template provided, outline the key shape with white royal icing using a No1 tube, except for the main part of the key handle which is piped using a No2 tube to make the unit less fragile.

7 Flood in the outline with white run-icing, then allow to dry.

8 When dry, paint the key with silver food colouring.

9 Prepare a cake card by covering with blue-coloured sugarpaste. Crimp the edges as shown to create an attractive finish.

10 Attach the prepared marzipan door to the cake portions with a little egg white or a few dabs of royal icing.

11 Attach a length of silver cake band around the edge of the cake.

12 Attach the decorated cake portion to the cake board with a dab of royal icing. Position and attach the key with tiny dabs of royal icing. Pipe a fine rope edging along the edge of the crimper work using a No1 tube and blue-coloured royal icing. Complete the novelty with a piped inscription or name as shown in the photograph. Use a No1 tube with brown-coloured royal icing. Alternatively the decorated cakes, without the cake card could be packed in attractive presentation boxes as a novel way of distributing the cake to guests after the celebrations.

Outline of door

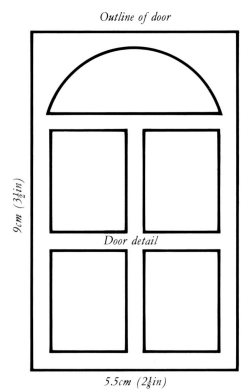

Door detail

$9cm\ (3\frac{1}{2}in)$

$5.5cm\ (2\frac{1}{8}in)$

Template for key

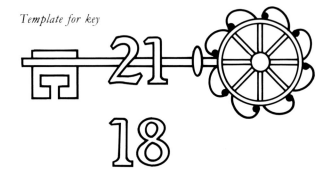

Love Birds

*Approximate
Height
of Cake
5cm (2in)*

*Approximate
Diameter
of Cake
11cm (4¹/4in)*

*Two cute little love birds exchanging their
engagement ring. This novel cake looks
good boxed with a matching gift tag.*

1 Cover a basic, round fruit cake approx 10 cm (4 ins) diameter with marzipan in the conventional manner. Then cover with pale, mint green-coloured sugarpaste, using the method described for anniversary cakes, see page 35.

2 Position the cake on a miniature cake card and attach a narrow length of silver cake band around the bottom edge. Secure the band to the cake with a thin line of royal icing.

3 Make the lace pieces for the cake side decoration. Using the patterns provided, place a piece of waxed paper over the design and pipe the heart shape first using a No1 tube and green royal icing. Then pipe the dot with a No0 tube and brown-coloured royal icing.
Note: When making lace pieces use freshly made royal icing, strengthened with a pinch of cream-of-tartar. Store the piped lace in a dry place away from any moisture and steam. Make plenty of extra pieces as they are very fragile.

4 Attach a narrow, green-coloured ribbon to the cake side. Carefully and gently remove the dry lace pieces from the waxed paper. Lift them up to the cake using a fine dry paintbrush and attach them, at an angle to the cake, with tiny dabs of royal icing. Again use freshly made icing to attach the lace pieces to the cake so that they will retain their position and dry rapidly.

5 Make the bird's wings and tail by rolling out some sugarpaste or flower paste and cutting out three triangles for each bird. Frill one edge of each triangle while it is still soft using the end of a wooden cocktail stick. Allow the parts to dry and then tint the frilled edges of the wings with edible green petal dust using a dry paintbrush.

6 To assemble the birds, model two balls of minty green-coloured sugarpaste – make one ball for the head slightly smaller than the other ball for the body. Whilst the paste is still soft insert the wings and tail into the body. Attach the head with royal icing and pipe the eyes in white and brown icing and pipe a white beak.

To finish the cake, position the birds onto the cake top and attach with royal icing. Attach the toy engagement ring into the birds' beaks with a dab of icing. Pipe an inscription with brown-coloured royal icing using a No1 or No0 tube.

Lettering

Engaged

Lace pieces for cake side

Straw Hat with Flowers

Approximate
Height
of Cake
4cm (1½in)

Approximate
Diameter
of Cake
13cm (5in)

*An easy-to-make straw hat featuring
piped buttercream flowers. This novelty is
suitable for Mother's Day, birthday
celebrations or Easter.*

1 Cover a basic, round cake with a thin layer of marzipan, or simply coat the top and sides of the cake with a thin coating of buttercream to seal the crumb and create a good base on which to pipe. Using the sequence illustrated above, pipe the sides of the hat with basket-weave using a No3 and No22 tube and chocolate- or coffee-coloured and flavoured buttercream.

2 Continuing with the basket-weave pattern, pipe the top of the hat. To make piping easier and more uniform, the cake top may be marked into divisions using the back of a small knife.

3 Finally, still using the basket-weave pattern, pipe the cake card to create the brim of the straw hat.

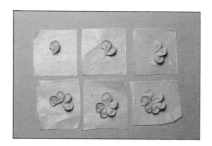

4 Pipe the daffodils using a No57, 58 or 59 petal tube and orangey yellow-coloured buttercream. Pipe the flowers on small, waxed paper squares placed on a flower nail.

5 Pipe the trumpet of the daffodil using a No2 tube and yellow buttercream; pipe as a spiral shape. Finish the flowers by edging the top of the trumpet with bright orange-coloured buttercream. Chill the flowers in the refrigerator ready for use, this makes them easier to handle when arranging and positioning them onto the cake.

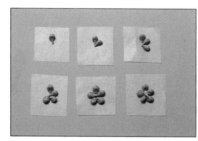

6 Using a No2 tube and violet-coloured buttercream, pipe the violets. Pipe five petals onto a small square of waxed paper; use a flower nail if preferred. Pipe in the centre using a No1 tube and bright yellow-coloured buttercream. Chill the finished violets along with the daffodils, ready for use.

7 Pipe out several leaves using a leaf tube, or by cutting the top from a conventional paper piping bag. Pipe the leaves onto waxed paper using a backwards and forwards shaking action to create the veins. Chill the leaves ready for use.

8 Remove the chilled flowers from the refrigerator and carefully release them from the waxed paper. Arrange the daffodils, violets and leaves on the prepared straw hat.

9 A small gift tag (see page 12) can be attached to the hat to mark the occasion.

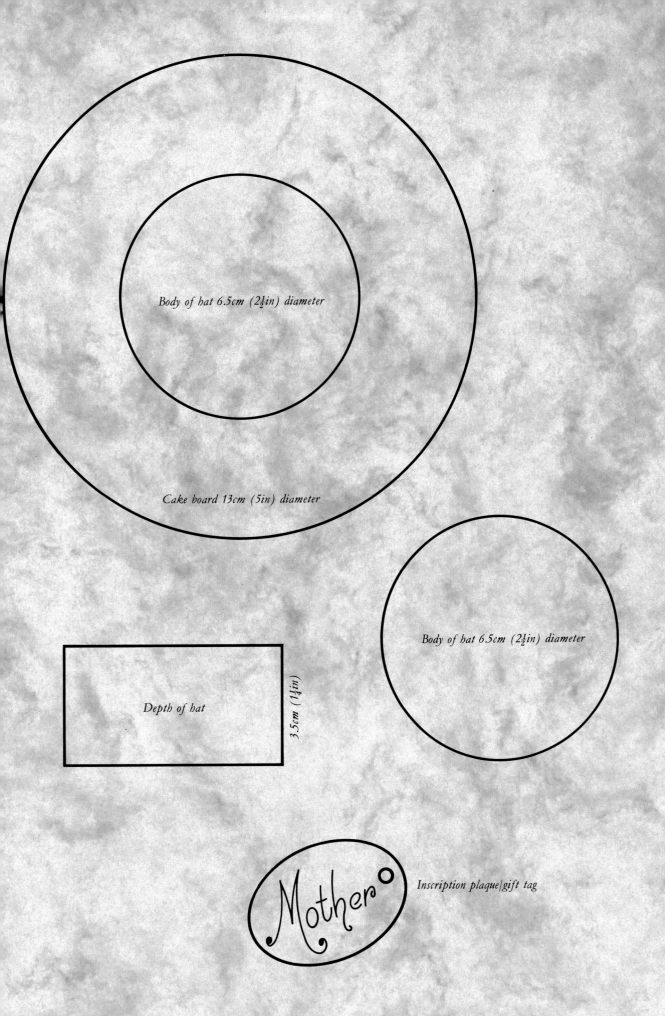

Body of hat 6.5cm (2½in) diameter

Cake board 13cm (5in) diameter

Depth of hat

3.5cm (1¾in)

Body of hat 6.5cm (2½in) diameter

Inscription plaque/gift tag

Strawberry
Punnet

Approximate
Height
of Punnet
4.2cm (1⅗in)
Plus Fruit

Approximate
Length
of Cake
8cm (3¼in)

A punnet of scrumptious marzipan
strawberries makes a novel feature for a
lazy, summer tea party.

Prepare the basic cake shape by cutting slanting sides on an oblong block of cake.

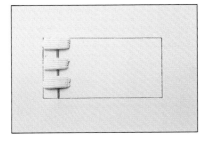

1 Make the sides of the strawberry punnet. Trace the templates provided onto drawing paper. Colour some royal icing dark brown and some a straw colour; make the straw colour by mixing small amounts of yellow, tangerine and brown food colouring. Place a piece of waxed paper over the drawing and pipe out the basket-weave work using tube No22 with straw-coloured icing, and tube No2 with brown icing. Start off by piping a straight line a short way in from the edge of the template, then pipe short bands of icing over the line at regular intervals. The spacing between the bands should be equal to the width of the piping.

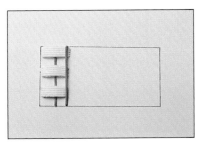

2 Pipe a second straight, vertical line of brown icing down the ends of the bands of straw-coloured icing.

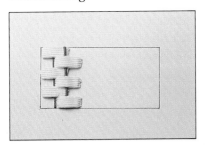

3 Pipe a second set of bands, this time positioning them in-between the previous set.

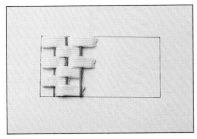

4 Pipe a third brown line as before and a third set of straw-coloured bands. Continue piping using this sequence until the shape is completed. Allow to dry flat.

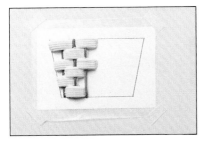

5 For the two punnet ends, pipe as for the sides but the first set of bands and the last set will have to taper to fit the shape.

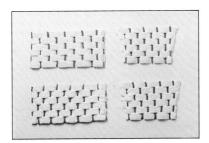

6 The four finished basket-weave sides. Allow them to dry completely before assembling.

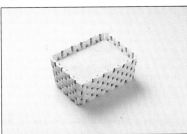

7 When dry, remove the piped sides from the waxed paper and attach to the cake with royal icing. The top of the punnet may be brushed with a little melted chocolate to seal the crumb.

8 Model the strawberries. Roll out a long, fat sausage of red-coloured marzipan, cut into equal sections and mould each piece into a ball shape. Form the balls into pear shapes and indent the top (wide end) with a little pressure from your finger. To create the texture on the strawberries, roll each one over the surface of a lemon grater.

9 For the hull, roll out a thin rope of green marzipan, cut into small pieces and roll into balls. Roll the balls into long strands, pointed at each end, cut a few of these in half. Using the blunt end of a paintbrush, pick up two full strands and a half strand creating a star pattern. Press the hull into the strawberry and remove the paintbrush.

10 Pipe tiny seeds on the strawberries using a No1 tube and straw-coloured royal icing. To make the finished strawberry look realistic, varnish with edible confectioner's varnish. Arrange a pile of strawberries in the punnet and finish with a gold band and bow. A greeting gift tag could also be added. This novelty is ideal for displaying in a presentation box when used as a gift.

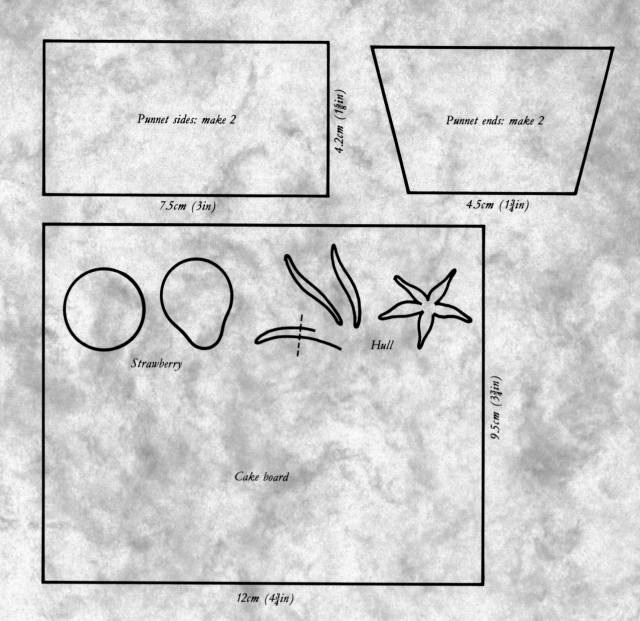

Punnet sides: make 2

4.2cm (1⅝in)

7.5cm (3in)

Punnet ends: make 2

4.5cm (1¾in)

Strawberry

Hull

Cake board

9.5cm (3¾in)

12cm (4¾in)

Parasol with
Flowers

Approximate
Height
of Cake
12.5cm (4⁷/₈in)

Approximate
Diameter
of Cake
8.5cm (3¹/₂in)

*As delicious as it is delightful, everyone
will simply adore this beautiful, flower-
filled parasol. It would also make a
delicate centrepiece for wedding reception
tables.*

1 Cover the basic cake shape with marzipan. Use a large circle of marzipan attached to the cake with apricot jam (jelly). Smooth the covering with your hands and a little icing (confectioner's) sugar to achieve a good finish. Cover the flat base of the dome as well.

2 Using the same procedure, cover the shape with a circle of pale pink sugarpaste. Stick the paste to the marzipan with egg white or spirit. Make indentations on the parasol, marking it into eight sections. Cover the flat base of the dome with white sugarpaste.

3 Cover a small cake card with pink sugarpaste to match the colour of the parasol. Brush the cake card lightly with egg white to stick the paste in place. Make a decorative edge to the board using marzipan crimpers.

4 Attach the prepared parasol base to the sugarpaste-covered card at an angle. Secure with royal icing and support with small blocks of polystyrene (styrofoam) until firm.

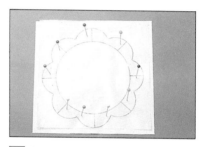

5 Make the parasol frill edging. Trace the template provided, transfer onto a work board and place a piece of waxed paper over the design. Make a second copy of the design, this time on greaseproof or tracing paper. Place this piece over a piece of tulle and pin together. Cut out the pattern and place the resulting tulle shape over the waxed paper on the work board, then secure taut with glass-headed pins.

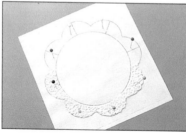

6 Using a No1 tube with white royal icing, pipe filigree over the tulle, then edge with a small plain shell. Pipe a plain shell along the straight lines in the design. Note: To strengthen the icing for filigree on tulle work, add a pinch of cream-of-tartar to the icing, which should be freshly made for this purpose.

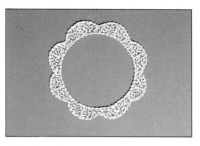

7 The finished tulle piece should be kept in a dry environment; do not keep in a moist, steamy kitchen.

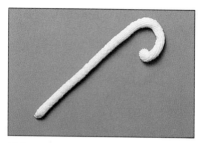

8 Make the parasol handle, using the template provided placed underneath a piece of waxed paper. Pipe out the shape using a No44 tube and white royal icing

9 When the handle shape is dry, decorate with narrow, pink ribbon twisted along the length and secured with a dab of royal icing. Attach the handle to the parasol with royal icing. Make a decorative bow from the same ribbon and tie to the handle once it is attached to the parasol.

10 Model some roses and leaves from sugarpaste or marzipan, tinting them with edible petal dust. Alternatively, you could purchase ready made edible or silk flowers.

11 Make some tulle fillers for the flower arrangement by cutting out small circles of tulle, pinching them together in the centre and twisting a flower wire around the middle to secure. Trim off the unwanted wire as you use them.

12 Using a similar technique to that described for the tulle fillers, make some ribbon fillers with coloured, narrow ribbon.

13 Arrange the flowers, leaves, tulle fillers and ribbons around the parasol handle to create an attractive and pleasing effect.

An edible gift tag with a piped greeting message would make the parasol with flowers more personalized.

Template for filigree parasol frill

Handle

Parasol depth 4cm (1½in)

Cake board diameter 10cm (4in)

Diameter 8.5cm (3½in)

Parasol: divide into eight

Train Engine

*Approximate
Height
of Cake
5cm (2in)*

*Approximate
Length
of Cake
9.5cm (3⅛in)*

*A miniature train engine decorated in
brightly-coloured marzipan would be well
appreciated at any birthday party, or even
given as a Father's Day gift.*

Prepare the necessary cake shapes cutting from a sheet of baked cake. The cake sections may be chilled a little to ease handling.

1 Cover the base of the train with green-coloured marzipan. The base of the shape has been coated with melted chocolate to firm-up the unit and make it sufficiently stable to hold the other cake shapes that will be positioned on top of it.

2 Cover the sides of the cabin shape with green marzipan; the top can be covered in green or gold marzipan. Using the template provided, cut out the cabin roof from black-coloured, rib-rolled marzipan or sugarpaste. Allow the roof to dry.

3 Attach the cabin to the train base with a little royal icing.

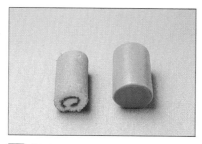

4 Make the engine boiler. Trim a mini Swiss roll to the required size and cover the sides and one end with green marzipan.

5 Attach the boiler of the engine to the train with a little royal icing.

6 Attach the cabin roof with royal icing.

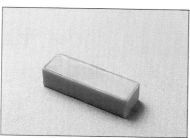

7 Cover a bar of cake with green marzipan. This will form a plinth on which to position the body of the train. If your cake is particularly fragile and crumbly, a coating of melted chocolate over the cake may be advisable to make a firmer plinth.

8 Position the train engine on the plinth, attaching with royal icing to secure.

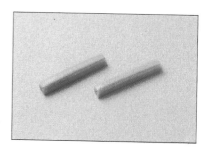

9 Make the corner sections from green marzipan, cut to size using the templates provided.

10 Attach the corner sections to the train with egg white.

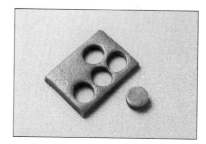

11 Roll out some dark brown marzipan, and cut out eight wheels using a small food cutter. Measure the exact depth of your cake plinth and use a cutter of a similar size for the wheels. Allow the shapes to firm-up.

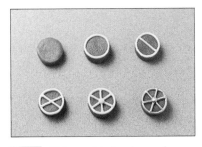

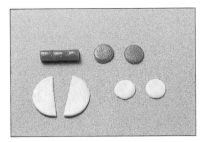

Using a No1 tube and bright red-orange icing, pipe the livery design on the engine. A sugarpaste inscription plaque may also be added along with the age of the recipient, piped on the cabin sides.

12 Using a No2 tube and royal icing, pipe the detail on the wheels. Allow the piped lines to dry, and then paint them with gold food colouring. Allow to dry.

14 Model the buffers from red marzipan, cutting out two small round discs using the end of a piping tube. Cut and halve a circle of yellow sugarpaste for the large windows. Two small circles of yellow paste make the small front windows.

13 Model a funnel from brown marzipan and place on a cocktail stick to firm-up without damaging its shape. Allow to dry. Pipe on the detail using a No2 tube and royal icing; allow to dry. Paint the piped lines with gold food colouring; dry.

15 Attach the funnel, wheels and windows to the train, securing each with dabs of royal icing.

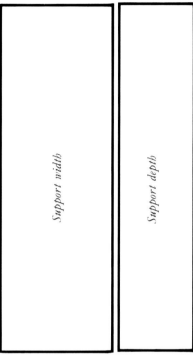

Support width   *Support depth*

9.5cm (3⅝in)   3cm (1¼in)   2cm (¾in)

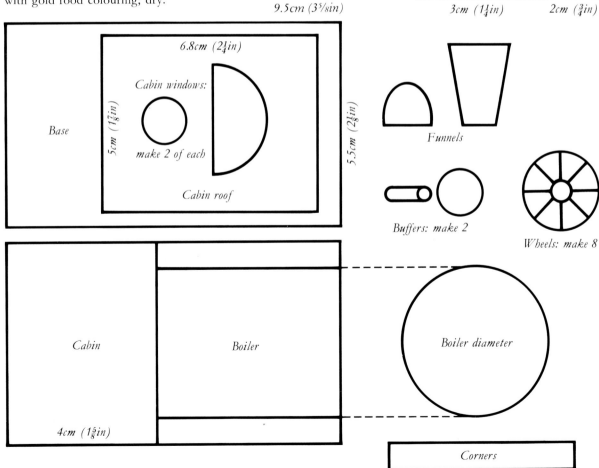

Base

6.8cm (2¼in)

Cabin windows:

5cm (1⅞in)

make 2 of each

Cabin roof

5.5cm (2⅛in)

Funnels

Buffers: make 2

Wheels: make 8

Cabin   *Boiler*   *Boiler diameter*

4cm (1⅝in)

Corners

Oven Finished Cakes

Approximate
Height
of Cakes
5cm (2in)

Approximate
Diameter
of Cakes
10cm (4in)

*Rich fruit cakes with traditional oven
finished decoration – always a most
welcome tea-time treat.*

Simnel Cake

This traditional Easter Sunday cake is a rich, fruit cake baked with a disc of marzipan through the middle of the cake. Allow the cake to cool and remove it from the tin or hoop.

1 Prepare a thick disc of yellow marzipan to the same diameter as the cake. Brush the top of the cake with boiled apricot jam (jelly) and secure the marzipan disc onto the cake.

2 Mark a diamond pattern on the soft marzipan using the back of a knife. Make eleven small balls of marzipan, to represent the loyal apostles. Brush the marzipan top with egg white and arrange the balls around the top edge of the cake. Brush the balls with egg white.

3 Toast the marzipan under a hot grill for about 30 seconds or until the sugar caramelizes and the marzipan takes on a golden brown colour.
Note: Leaving the greaseproof (waxed) paper (used to line the cake tin) on the cake will help to protect the sides from scorching. Allow the cake to cool.

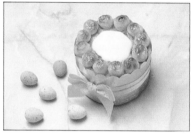

4 Spoon or pipe a little glacé icing into the centre of the cake top and decorate with three sugar-coated, miniature Easter eggs, or a small modelled marzipan chick.

Dundee Cake

Again a rich, fruit cake recipe is used, usually omitting the cherries and replacing with other fruit. Before baking the cakes, the tops are decorated with blanched, split almonds arranged in a circular pattern around the edge of the cake as shown. When baked and cooled you may like to decorate the sides of the cake with a coloured foil band. The cakes can then be wrapped in clear cellophane and finished with an attractive tartan ribbon and bow. Write a greetings message on a small gift tag made to match the tartan ribbon by sticking ribbon onto thin card and cutting out to the required shape and size.

Witchy
Chocolate Cake

Approximate
Height
of Cake
13.5cm (5¼in)

Approximate
Width
of Cake
7.5cm (3in)

*Delicious chocolate cake masquerading in
the guise of a witch. Let the children have
a go at making their own quick-to-
decorate hallowe'en treats.*

1 Prepare a chocolate cake base to the size of the template provided. Two witches can be made from one long oblong sheet of cake, by simply reversing the template.
Coat the cake in chocolate by placing the cake on a cooling wire with waxed paper beneath, spread the back with melted chocolate and allow to set. Turn the cake over and cover the sides and the top with melted chocolate, then tap the wire to encourage the excess chocolate to drain away. Allow the chocolate to partially set and then remove the cake from the wire. Place onto waxed or greaseproof paper to finish setting.

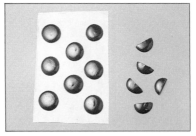

2 Pipe chocolate drops onto waxed paper using the template provided as a size guide. Allow to set, then cut the drops in half.

3 Dip the straight edge of the chocolate drop halves into melted chocolate and attach them to the witch's body. Place a row of drops around the base and another row about one-third of the way down from the point to give the appearance of a hat.

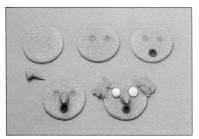

4 Roll out some green-coloured sugarpaste to about 3mm ($\frac{1}{8}$in) thick; adding a touch of blue colour in with the green gives a better colour for the witch's face. Cut out a circle using a round cutter of the required size. Indent the eyes with a modelling tool and using a ball modelling tool, press a small ball of red marzipan in place for the mouth. Add a pointed nose, attaching with egg white, and then pipe in the eyes with white- and brown-coloured royal icing. The hair is made by pressing egg-yellow-coloured marzipan through a fine sieve, tea-strainer or clay gun. Attach two tufts of hair, using a little egg white to secure.

5 Model a hand from a pear-shaped piece of green marzipan, making a cut to represent the thumb; allow to firm-up. Model the broom from thin strands of brown marzipan attached together with a little egg white and allowed to dry.
Attach the prepared face, broom and hand to the witch's body with royal icing. A small, sugarpaste star and moon motif attached to the hat with royal icing may also be added.

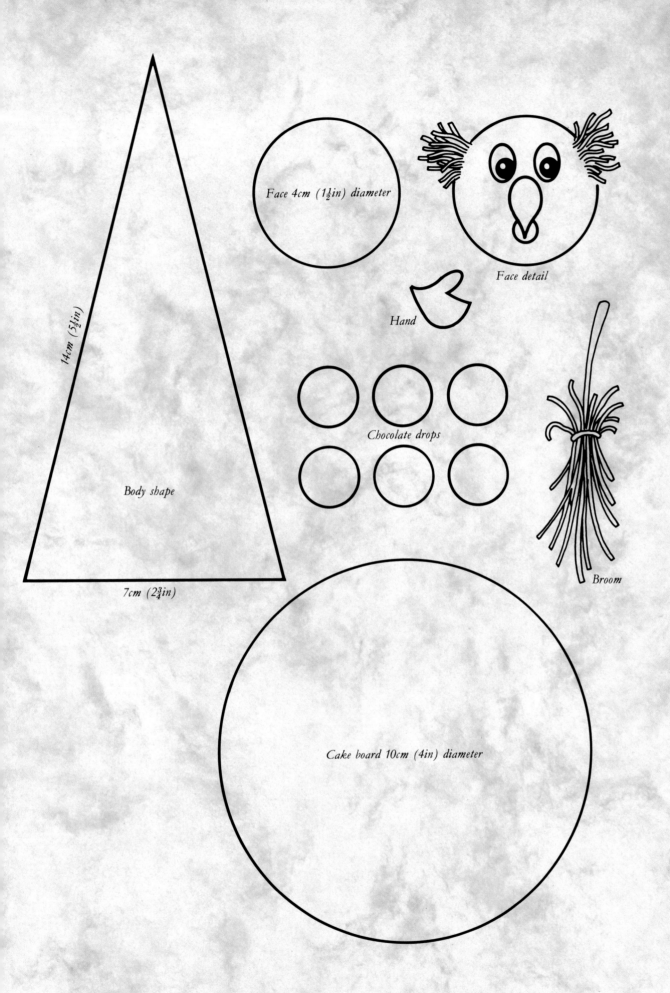

Face 4cm (1½in) diameter

Face detail

Hand

14cm (5½in)

Body shape

7cm (2¾in)

Chocolate drops

Broom

Cake board 10cm (4in) diameter

Firework Party

*Approximate
Length
of Box
8cm (3¹/₄in)*

*Approximate
Width
of Box
6cm (2¹/₄in)*

*Add a sparkle to your celebration table
with this colourful box of marzipan
firecrackers.*

Prepare the basic cake shape from a small oblong of sponge. Layer the cake with jam (jelly) and cream, if desired. This novelty could also be made from rich fruit cake; bake, (or cut out from a slab) to the required shape and size, then marzipan in the conventional manner.

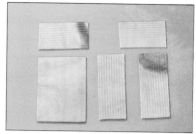

1 Partly mix some brown, yellow and orange marzipan or sugarpaste to create a streaky, boxwood effect. Roll the paste out to approximately 3mm ($\frac{1}{8}$in) thick, then rib-roll the paste to create an interesting texture. Using the templates provided, cut out the required shapes for the firework box. Allow the shapes to dry and firm-up.

2 Attach the box sides to the prepared cake using royal icing.

3 Using the lettering style provided, cut a stencil from re-usable, oiled parchment, or from thin card. Place the prepared stencil on the lid of the box and spread across a thin layer of black- or dark brown-coloured royal icing. Carefully remove the stencil to reveal the inscription 'FIREWORKS'.

4 Make the fireworks. For the triangular-shaped firework, roll out some orange-coloured marzipan, make some small balls of red-coloured marzipan and press onto the rolled surface. Roll out further to flatten the balls and create a spotted pattern.

5 Using the template provided, cut out a circle of the paste, then divide and cut into eight sections. Cut as shown around the edge of the circle to give each section a straight edge. Separate the sections and place onto waxed paper to dry.

6 Assemble three triangles together with royal icing to make the firework. Pipe on the touch paper using a No2 tube with blue-coloured royal icing.

7 Roll out two fat sausage shapes of blue- and red-coloured marzipan.

8 Cut each roll into four sections using a moist knife, then re-rolling the pieces to keep them round in shape. Using a little egg white, assemble by alternating two red and two blue discs to form two striped fireworks. Pipe a blue touch paper on each.

9 Roll out two thin sausage shapes, one of yellow and one of green marzipan. Twist the two rolls together and re-roll to create a spiral striped pattern. Cut to the required length to make a firework and pipe a blue icing touch paper on each to complete.

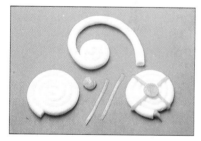

10 For the Catherine wheel, roll out a long sausage of white sugarpaste and then roll into a spiral to form a circle. Decorate the firework with thin crossed strips of yellow marzipan and position a small blue circle in the centre. Pipe a blue icing touch paper.

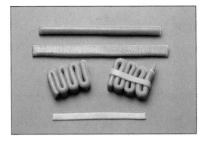

11 The jumping Jack is made from a long sausage of light brown-coloured marzipan or sugarpaste. Flatten the roll and then fold up as shown. Finish the firework with a thin strip of green marzipan attached with a little egg white. A blue icing touch paper completes the firework.

12 To decorate the box of fireworks when assembled, cut out some white and yellow star shapes from thinly rolled sugarpaste.
Arrange the fireworks and stars in the box, securing with dabs of royal icing. Position the lid at the side of the box when displaying the novelty.

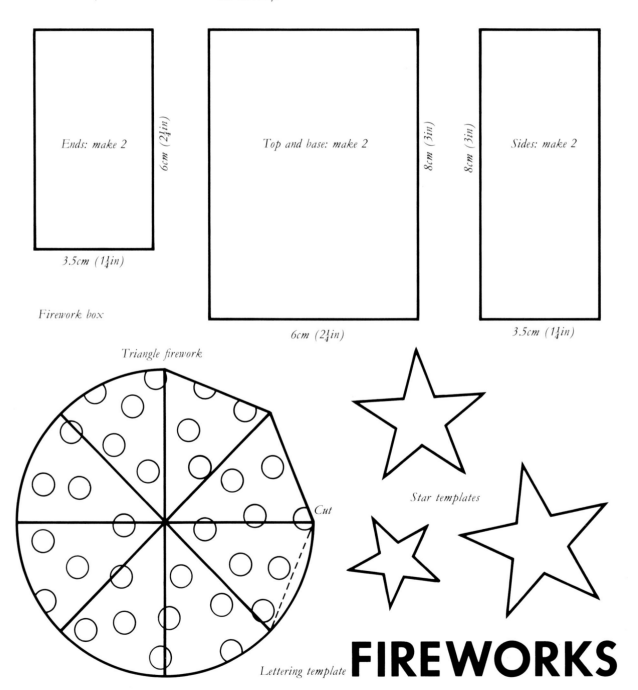

Ends: make 2

6cm (2¼in)

3.5cm (1¼in)

Firework box

Top and base: make 2

8cm (3in)

6cm (2¼in)

8cm (3in)

Sides: make 2

3.5cm (1¼in)

Triangle firework

Cut

Star templates

Lettering template **FIREWORKS**

Green Tortoise

Approximate
Height
of Cake
5cm (2in)

Approximate
Diameter
of Cake
9cm (3½in)

*This novelty cake will be admired by all
ages. Display the tortoise in an attractive
presentation box with a gift tag carrying
a greeting message.*

1 Cover the basic dome-shaped cake with marzipan. Roll out the marzipan and cut-out a large circle, attaching it to the cake with apricot jam (jelly). Notice that a portion of cake has been cut away to allow for the neck of the tortoise. Smooth the shape with your hands which have been dusted with a little icing (confectioner's) sugar to create a good finish.

2 Next cover the marzipanned cake with pale green-coloured sugarpaste. Stick the paste to the marzipan with egg white or spirit. Using the Garrett frill principle edge the dome with a frill of green sugarpaste. To make the frill, roll out the coloured paste and cut using a large, round, fluted cutter. Remove a circle of paste from the shape, cut and open out to form a strip. Roll the end of a cocktail stick along the edge of the frill with gentle and even pressure to create a ruffle effect. Work quickly as the paste will soon crust and crack. Attach the frill to the tortoise as soon as possible, sticking with a little egg white or spirit.

3 Decorate the join between the frill and the cake with a crimper pattern. Position small pieces of wooden dowel, as shown, to make spaces for the feet and allow the frill to curve naturally over them. Also work the frill around the aperture made for the head.

4 Once the paste frill has dried completely, highlight the edge of the frill with a darker shade of edible, green petal dust applied with a soft, dry paintbrush.

5 For the shell pattern, roll out some yellow and some dark brown-coloured marzipan. Layer the two colours together, sticking with egg white if necessary. Roll up the marzipan Swiss roll fashion. Allow the roll to firm a little.

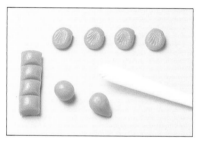

6 Cut thin slices from the roll of marzipan to create circular pieces with a spiral pattern on each. Stick the circles onto the body of the tortoise using a little egg white or spirit.

7 Roll out four balls of coffee-coloured marzipan for the feet. Shape the balls into pear shapes, and then mark on the detail using a modelling tool.

8 Make the head from a larger ball of coffee-coloured marzipan. Indent the eyes with a modelling tool and cut out a thin wedge for the mouth. Hold the mouth open until dry by replacing the removed wedge covered with a folded square of waxed paper. Model a tail for the tortoise.

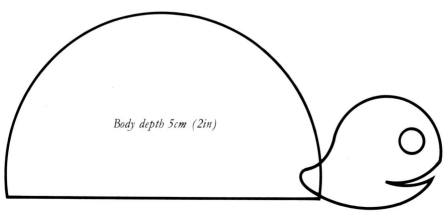

Body depth 5cm (2in)

9 Model a hat for the tortoise from black marzipan. Make a drum shape from a flattened ball of marzipan, and the brim from a thinly flattened ball, then attach the two together with egg white. Using royal icing, attach the head, feet and tail to the body of the tortoise. Stick the hat onto the head with egg white. Pipe in the eyes with white and brown royal icing and add a marzipan nose. The hat may then be decorated with a sugar flower.

Template for frill edging

Head

Shell markings

Feet

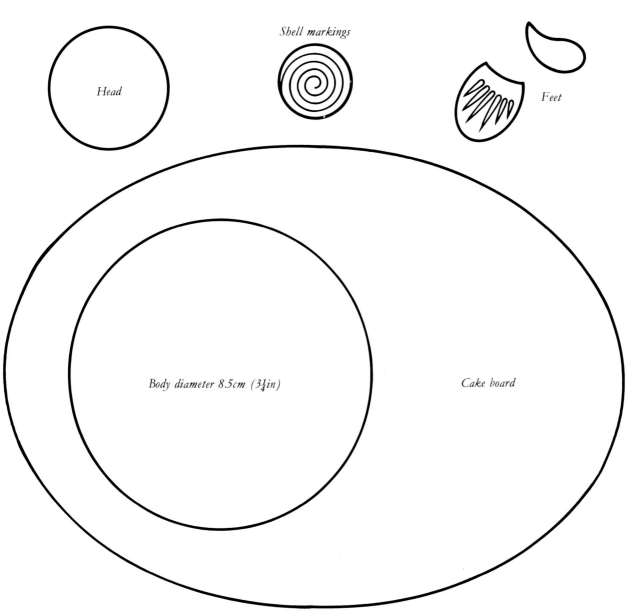

Body diameter 8.5cm (3¼in)

Cake board

New Year Clock

*Approximate
Height
of Cake
11.5cm (4½in)*

*Approximate
Diameter
of Cake
9cm (3½in)*

*Ring in the new with this realistic edible
alarm clock, complete with alarm bells
ready to ring at midnight!*

1 Cover the top, base and sides of a basic round cake with marzipan. Next cover the top and base only with white sugarpaste. Roll out the paste, cut out two circles and stick them to the marzipan with egg white. Now cover the sides of the clock cake by rolling out a long strip of marzipan, attaching to the cake with egg white. The marzipan used for the clock is streaked to create a more interesting finish to the clock. Make the streaked marzipan by partly mixing together two or three colours of marzipan, those used here were orange, brown and yellow.

2 Use the template provided to transfer the numerals onto the clock face. Pipe the numerals with black-coloured royal icing using a No1 tube.

3 For the alarm bells, thinly roll some sugarpaste and cut out two circles. Use the circles of sugarpaste to line the two halves of a cut table tennis ball. Allow the paste shapes to dry, remove them from the formers and then paint the outside with gold food colouring.

4 Make the clock hands from black-coloured marzipan. Make two thin rolls, of differing lengths, two carrot-shaped tops, and a small disc for the centre.

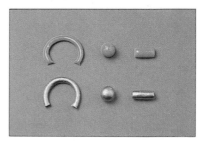

5 To make the clock handle and feet, first mould a long sausage of marzipan. Cut off two lengths to support the bells, two feet and form two small balls. Also prepare a short length for the handle and bend into shape. Allow the shapes to firm-up and then paint with gold food colouring.

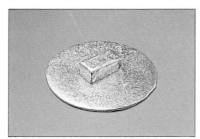

6 Prepare a cake card on which to assemble and present the finished clock cake. Cut a small block of wood, or use a block of firmed-up marzipan, and cover with board covering foil. If you are unable to obtain small gold cake cards, make using silver foil and then paint with gold food colouring to match the cake accessories.

7 Position the body of the clock on the prepared card and secure with royal icing. Support the clock with blocks of polystyrene (styrofoam) until set. Attach the handle, bell supports and feet, sticking with royal icing. Small dabs of white royal icing are used to attach the clock hands to the face, positioning them just around midnight.

8 Attach the prepared alarm bells with royal icing.

9 Make the holly leaves. Thinly roll out some green-coloured sugarpaste. Cut out the leaf shapes with a cutter. Mark the veins on the leaves with a small knife or modelling tool. Place the leaves onto a piece of crumpled foil; this will create a natural curve to the leaves. Allow to dry. When dry, add further colour to the leaves by applying tones of orange and moss-green edible petal dust using a dry paintbrush. Make several small holly berries from small balls of red-coloured marzipan. Arrange and attach the prepared holly leaves and berries around the top and base of the clock.

Clock diameter 8cm (3in)

Numerals for clock face

12 11 1 10 2 9 3 8 4 7 5 6

Legs

Handle

Cake board 10cm (4in) diameter

Holly leaf template

Clock hands